Enigma Books

Also published by Enigma Books

Hitler's Table Talk: 1941–1944
In Stalin's Secret Service
Hitler and Mussolini: The Secret Meetings
The Jews in Fascist Italy: A History
The Man Behind the Rosenbergs
Roosevelt and Hopkins: An Intimate History
Diary 1937–1943 (Galeazzo Ciano)
Secret Affairs: FDR, Cordell Hull, and Sumner Welles
Hitler and His Generals: Military Conferences 1942–1945
Stalin and the Jews: The Red Book
The Secret Front: Nazi Political Espionage
Fighting the Nazis: French Intelligence and Counterintelligence
A Death in Washington: Walter G. Krivitsky and the Stalin Terror
The Battle of the Casbah: Terrorism and Counterterrorism in Algeria
1955–1957
Hitler's Second Book: The Unpublished Sequel to *Mein Kampf*
At Napoleon's Side in Russia: The Classic Eyewitness Account
The Atlantic Wall: Hitler's Defenses for D-Day
Double Lives: Stalin, Willi Münzenberg, and the Seduction of the
Intellectuals
France and the Nazi Threat: The Collapse of French Diplomacy 1932–
1939
Mussolini: The Secrets of His Death
Top Nazi: Karl Wolff—The Man Between Hitler and Himmler
Empire on the Adriatic: Mussolini's Conquest of Yugoslavia
The Origins of the War of 1914 (3-volume set)
Hitler's Foreign Policy 1933–1939: The Road to World War II
The Origins of Fascist Ideology 1918–1925
Max Corvo: OSS Italy 1942–1945
Hitler's Contract: The Secret History of the Italian Edition of *Mein Kampf*
Secret Intelligence and the Holocaust
Israel at High Noon
Balkan Inferno
Hollywood's Celebrity Gangster
Calculated Risk
The Murder of Maxim Gorky
The Kravchenko Case
The Mafia and the Allies

Georges Poisson

Hitler's Gift to France

The Return of the Remains of Napoleon II

Crisis at Vichy - December 15, 1940

Translated by Robert L. Miller

Enigma Books

Copyright © 2008 Enigma Books
Original Title: *Le retour des cendres de l'Aiglon*
Published by: Nouveau Monde Editions

Translated by Robert L. Miller

ISBN-13: 978-1-929631-67-4

Printed in the United States of America

Library of Congress Cataloging-in-Publication Data
Poisson, Georges, 1924-
  [Retour des cendres de l'Aiglon. English]
  Hitler's gift to France : the return of the remains of Napoleon II / Georges Poisson ; translated by Robert L. Miller.

  p. : ill. ; cm.

  Includes bibliographical references and index.
  Translation of: Le retour des cendres de l'Aiglon.
  ISBN-13: 978-1-929631-67-4
  ISBN-10: 1-929631-67-7

1. France--History--German occupation, 1940-1945. 2. Bonaparte, François-Charles-Joseph, Herzog von Reichstadt, 1811-1832--Death and burial. 3. France--Politics and government--1940-1945. 4. France--Foreign relations--Germany. 5. Germany--Foreign relations--France. 6. Hitler, Adolf, 1889-1945. 7. Laval, Pierre, 1883-1945. 8. Pétain, Philippe, 1856-1951. I. Miller, Robert L. (Robert Lawrence), 1945- Title. III. Title: Retour des cendres de l'Aiglon

DC397 .P59313 2007
944.081/6

Contents

Translator's Note

Throughout this book the son of Napoleon I and Archduchess Marie Louise of Habsbourg, by his full name Napoleon François Joseph Charles, is referred to by several different titles: known at his birth in 1811 as the King of Rome (Roi de Rome), at Napoleon's abdication on June 22, 1815, he was confirmed Emperor of the French as Napoleon II for two weeks until the return of King Louis XVIII and the restoration of the Bourbon dynasty. Taken by his mother to Vienna he would thereafter be called by his princely Austrian title of Duke of Reichstadt, used in all official Austrian and German communications including those by Adolf Hitler. At the Habsbourg court and among the Viennese he was known affectionately as Franz. The popular legend of Napoleon's son as the young eagle, the *Aiglon* or "Eaglet" and the well-known play by Edmond Rostand *L'Aiglon* remains his most endearing name in French popular history. The literature of the period and historical studies generally use the official name and title of Duke of Reichstadt.

Introduction

Napoleon, Hitler, and Pétain

It was a bitterly cold December night. The Seine was almost completely frozen, something Paris had not seen in recent memory. Since late October France was in the grip of a numbing cold spell and the main problem for most Parisians besides finding enough to eat was to keep warm. Around midnight, as a thick snow began to cover the streets and rooftops, an extraordinary event took place known only to a handful of people.

During the final hours of December 14, 1940, a cortège of horses pulling an artillery carriage with a heavy casket covered by a black cloth and flanked by German soldiers in jackboots, helmets and full winter dress uniforms, filed quietly through the empty streets. They marched from the Gare de l'Est down the deserted boulevards, across the river and over to the left bank past the Eiffel Tower to the esplanade of the monumental mausoleum of Emperor Napoleon I under the dome of the

Invalides. One hundred years to the day since the return of the Emperor's ashes in 1840, the remains of the son of Napoleon I and Empress Marie Louise of Habsbourg, known officially as the Duke of Reichstadt, were being suddenly returned to France to rest permanently next to the father he barely knew.

Napoleon Bonaparte, defeated at Waterloo, died in his British exile on the island of Saint Helena in the South Atlantic in 1821. Upon his abdication on June 22, 1815, Napoleon had willed the French Empire to his son who was barely five years old. The young boy had technically only reigned over France for two weeks as Napoleon II when the Bourbon kings reclaimed the French throne. Less than twenty years after his death, the cult of Napoleon had grown to such proportions in France that King Louis-Philippe, after delicate negotiations with the English government, secured Lord Palmerston's approval for a French naval expedition to bring Napoleon's remains back to Paris. This happened in an atmosphere of incredible enthusiasm in a famous ceremony on December 15, 1840. The Emperor was later buried in the Invalides in his permanent tomb, a magnificent sarcophagus of pink porphyry. After the Bourbon restoration the young Napoleon II was raised at court in Vienna as an Austrian prince but he died of tuberculosis in 1832 at age 21. He was buried in Vienna in the Habsburg family crypt and all but forgotten except for a handful of French Bonapartists and the imperial nobility that cherished the memory of the unhappy prince, a mere shadow in France's turbulent history.

Within a few years the cult of Napoleon, father and son, acquired a new dimension with the publication of several memoirs by members of the Emperor's entourage and principally the two volumes by Count Emmanuel de Las Cases *Mémorial de Sainte Hélène*, one of the great publishing successes of the nineteenth century first published in 1823. The nostalgic movement that rested on the military glory of the Napoleonic wars created a powerful popular myth that would eventually play a major role in the creation of the Second Empire under Napoleon III.[1] Prince Louis-Napoleon Bonaparte, a nephew of Napoleon I, was elected president of the Second Republic and instigated a coup d'état in 1851 transforming the republic into a restored empire. In 1870 France was quickly defeated by Prussia in a lightning campaign that ended with the capture and abdication of Napoleon III, the searing loss of the two provinces of Alsace-Lorraine and the founding of the Third Republic in 1871. The Napoleonic dream was finally over but the power of the imagery and the cult of imperial glory would linger on.

The catastrophic defeat of the French army and the British Expeditionary Force by Germany in May and June 1940 ranks as one of modern history's most sweeping military and political collapses of a great power. In June 1940, for the second time in seventy years, after the victory of 1918 in the First World War, France was forced to surrender to Nazi Germany. The immediate consequences of those cataclysmic six weeks in May and June went far beyond the humiliating surrender and the armistice. They triggered events that would alter the course of history: the creation of the Vichy government under Marshal Philippe Pétain, the resistance of General Charles de Gaulle, the reelection of Franklin D. Roosevelt to a third term, Hitler's failure to defeat Great Britain, and the realization by the end of the summer that the war would continue with no clear end in sight. While eminent historians have analyzed and explained the larger picture a few unsolved mysteries remain, the return of the remains of *L'Aiglon* certainly being one of them.

Historians of Vichy generally dedicate a few short lines to what appeared as an incomprehensible personal decision by Adolf Hitler within the larger picture of the German victory and occupation of France. The connection between the return of the

---

1. Louis-Napoleon Bonaparte born in 1808 was the son of Hortense de Beauharnais, a daughter of Josephine, Napoleon's first wife, and of Louis Bonaparte, a younger brother of the Emperor, who became King of Holland.

Duke of Reichstadt's remains and the political crisis at Vichy has never been adequately explained.[2] The secret announcement by Deputy Prime Minister Pierre Laval to Marshal Pétain and his entourage of Hitler's decision to approve the return of Napoleon II triggered a palace conspiracy leading to the dramatic dismissal and arrest of the Deputy Prime Minister on December 13. It was a show of power politics and possibly independence by the Vichy leadership prompted by the dramatic announcement of the return of the ashes of the Duke of Reichstadt set for December 15, 1940.

This study by Georges Poisson, an eminent Napoleonic specialist and art historian of the monuments of Paris, finally explains one of the remaining enigmas in the history of World War II. While working on his earlier book about the return of the ashes of the Emperor Napoleon I in 1840, the author discovered a number of related documents in the archives regarding Napoleon II that led him to publish this amazing book.[3] There were many indications that the return of the remains of the Duke of Reichstadt, while a defeated France was at its lowest point under virtually total German control, was not an isolated and mysterious operation as it is usually described. The elaborate plans to bring the casket of Napoleon's heir to

2. Robert O. Paxton *Vichy Old Guard and New Order 1940–1944* (New York: A. Knopf, 1976); Julian Jackson *France: The Dark Years 1940–1945* (New York: Oxford, 2001); Walter L. Langer *Our Vichy Gamble* (New York: Knopf, 1947); Michael R. Marrus and Robert O. Paxton *Vichy France and the Jews* (New York: Basic Books, 1981); and Robert Aron *Histoire de Vichy* (Paris, 1954); Henri Michel *Vichy: Année 40* (Paris, 1966), J.P. Cointet *Histoire de Vichy*, (Paris, 2003) and *Pierre Laval* (Paris, 1993), J. P. Azéma and O. Wieviorka *Vichy 1940–1944*, Serge Klarsfeld *Vichy-Auschwitz* 2 vols. (Paris, 1983–1985) among many other French historians and researchers.
3. See Georges Poisson *L'Aventure du retour des cendres* (Paris: Tallandier, 2004) based on archival materials details the delicate international negotiations between France and England that allowed the return of the remains of Emperor Napoleon I from the island prison of Saint Helena in 1840. Among the many books on the subject it is the first to offer a detailed account of the diplomatic negotiations that took place.

Paris during the dismal winter of 1940 made little sense against the backdrop of the first six months of the Vichy government following the armistice. The interaction between the backroom struggle for power at Vichy and the ambiguities of the German occupation of France within the decision to return the remains of Napoleon's only son has remained unclear for over sixty-seven years and can finally be placed in the proper context.

Why would Adolf Hitler in the wake of his most spectacular military triumph and in the midst of what was becoming a world war suddenly decide, of all things, to offer to an utterly defeated and humiliated France under German military occupation what he thought was a spectacular and endearing gift?

Since his death in 1832 the Duke of Reichstadt was buried with the other Habsbourgs in the Crypt of the Capuchins in Vienna. On the night of December 15, 1940, the Duke's remains arrived at their final resting place next to his father Napoleon I under the magnificent Dôme of the Invalides. The event stands out as an odd and isolated moment in the history of Vichy France, a regime a number of historians and writers have described as only somewhat typical of the collaborationist governments set up by Nazi Germany in occupied Europe. The term "collaboration" itself conjures a long list of trademark Nazi brutalities that characterized the years of occupation: the early persecution of the Jews by both the Germans and Vichy, their deportation to death camps along with a long list of real and imagined enemies of Nazi Germany: Freemasons, Gaullists, members of so-called secret societies,[4] anti-Nazi socialists, German refugees in France and, after June 22, 1941, communists and members of the resistance, anyone critical of the authorities or listening to foreign broadcasts such as the BBC and so on

---

4. This could take on bizarre overtones as the Germans in Paris in June 1940 went around looking for the adherents of the universal language Esperanto considered the members of a dangerous secret society.

were placed on the Nazi lists.[5] But in December 1940 most of those horrors were still to come and an organized resistance to the German occupation was barely beginning.[6]

The Vichy government's four year existence can only be understood within the broader context of the Second World War and yet Hitler's decision to return the ashes of the Duke of Reichstadt to France seems to defy all explanations as an odd and strangely isolated event, during the late fall and winter of 1940.

The battle of France that began during the early hours of May 10 with the invasion of Luxembourg, Holland and Belgium was a major consideration in Franklin D. Roosevelt's decision to run for a third term.[7] As of May 8, 1940, Assistant Secretary of State and New Deal insider Adolf A. Berle wrote in his diary: "It is understood that Roosevelt, unless the situation changes, will wait until the last minute and then issue a statement in favor of Mr. Hull."[8] Washington's highest circles were convinced that the president was about to endorse Secretary of State Cordell Hull for the nomination at the Democratic Party convention in Chicago in July 1940 before retiring to private life at Hyde Park. But in less than one week, by May 15, the world situation would

---

5. According to research by Serge Klarsfeld there were 330,000 Jews living in France in 1940, of these 74,721 were deported to various concentration camps in Germany and Poland between 1941 and 1944 with only a handful alive at the end of the war.

6. For the early organized resistance to the German occupation in 1940 by French anti-Nazi army officers see Colonel Paul Paillole, *Fighting the Nazis* (New York: Enigma Books, 2003) and among the intellectuals the vivid description by Martin Blumenson, *The Vildé Affair. Beginnings of the French Resistance* (Boston: Houghton Mifflin, 1977).

7. "On January 24, 1940, over lunch with Morgenthau, FDR said: 'I do not want to run unless between now and the convention things get very, very much worse in Europe." Ted Morgan, *FDR* (New York: Simon and Shuster, 1985) p. 520. See also R. Dallek *Franklin D. Roosevelt and American Foreign Policy 1932–1945* (New York: Oxford, 1995).

8. A. A. Berle, *Navigating the Rapids 1918–1971. From the Papers of Adolf A. Berle* (New York: Harcourt, 1973) p. 311.

be so radically altered by the furious battle engaged in Luxembourg, Holland, Belgium, and northern France itself that FDR's plans for a return to private life had to change. Roosevelt had certainly considered such a scenario and determined that he must run for a third term when it became obvious that France was inevitably sliding into defeat.[9]

While the German army was violating the neutrality of Luxembourg, the Netherlands and Belgium, the best divisions of the French army were quickly crossing the border into Belgium and even venturing as far north as Holland. The spectacular German success in taking Fort Eben Emaël on May 11 and 12 forced the Belgians to fall back, effectively ensuring Belgium's collapse in a matter of days. But France's crack motorized units and cavalry were following General Maurice Gamelin's original plan to the letter. On May 13 and 14 Wehrmacht Panzers almost contemporaneously overwhelmed French positions at the key juncture of Sedan across the border from Luxembourg, an area no longer covered by the Maginot Line. The Germans broke through the French Second Army lines and immediately turned west toward the English Channel as the French and British armies, over 300,000 men, were progressively trapped in a shrinking pocket that was being pushed back towards the sea and a forced retreat towards Dunkirk. The miraculous evacuation to England would follow.

The remainder of the French army, unable to execute a maneuver to break the encirclement, was from that moment on fighting isolated and losing battles. The roads were clogged with some four million terrified refugees fleeing the German army's advance and a growing confusion preventing any effective military operations. Communications between the high command and units in the field were extremely faulty or totally

---

9. "By the beginning of the summer, 1940, I took it for granted that the President had decided it was his duty to accept he nomination." Sam Rosenman *Working With Roosevelt* (New York: Harper, 1952), p. 200.

nonexistent. On May 19, nine days into the German offensive, Prime Minister Paul Reynaud sacked his commander in chief General Maurice Gamelin and appointed General Maxime Weygand as supreme commander. By then the battle was already both strategically and tactically lost and the new commander was unable to reverse the trend as French army units were forced to fall back or surrender. Winston Churchill, who had become Prime Minister on May 9, was also powerless to stem the negative tide in France and withheld committing the Royal Air Force to the French front much to Reynaud and Weygand's despair. On June 10 Italy declared war on France and Great Britain, Mussolini's famous "stab in the back,"[10] as the French armies were fighting in isolated pockets behind Paris and resisting the Italian attacks on the Alps. Paris was declared an open city and occupied by the Wehrmacht without any fighting on June 14. The French government, repeating the historic moves of 1870 and 1914, left the capital for various locations in the Loire Valley until it finally reached Bordeaux.

Paul Reynaud resigned as Prime Minister on June 16 and was replaced by Marshal Pétain who formed a new government at the request of President Albert Lebrun. When the issue of the armistice came up a number of politicians and President Lebrun himself were ready to move the government to North Africa but the realistic possibility of being able to carry on the war and the determination of the pro-armistice faction in the government ended any such move.[11] Through Spanish Ambassador Lequerica, the Pétain government asked Germany for armistice

---

10. President Roosevelt in a famous commencement address at the University of Virginia was to say: "On this tenth day of June, 1940, the hand that held the dagger has struck it into the back of its neighbor."
11. The intrigues of Pierre Laval and Raphaël Alibert effectively stopped the move to North Africa. A few political leaders including Georges Mandel sailed to Morocco aboard the ship Massilia but were forcibly returned to France with tragic consequences. See William L. Shirer, *The Collapse of the Third Republic* (New York: Simon and Shuster, 1969) p. 862.

terms on the following day. The Germans had previously refused to discuss an armistice with the Belgian government requiring instead an unconditional surrender. But Hitler agreed to negotiate an armistice with France, a country that was after all a much bigger prize than Belgium. On the Axis side discussions between Hitler and Mussolini yielded a relatively lenient compromise compared to Germany's other conquered and occupied territories such as Poland. Upon the signing of both armistices, with the Germans at Compiègne on June 23, and with the Italians in Rome the next day, the French surrender became official on June 25. In less than two months France had dramatically and for many observers, incomprehensibly, lost the war and its status as a world power.[12]

In the mass confusion that swept the country very few Frenchmen heard the first appeal made by General Charles de Gaulle on June 18, 1940, in a BBC broadcast from London. De Gaulle had flown from Bordeaux to London in the same plane as General Spears on June 16. The Gaullist movement had very modest beginnings but its indomitable leader vowed to continue the fight and rejected the armistice. The decisions of the new French government became a major military and political issue for both the Allies and the Germans. The main points at stake were: the fate of France's powerful fleet, the world's third largest at the time, that was intact and had virtually not seen action in the battles of 1940; and the loyalty of France's vast colonial empire that was also unscathed by the six weeks of war.

---

12. J.-B. Duroselle, *L'Abîme. Politique étrangère de la France 1939–1944* (Paris: Imprimerie Nationale, 1982) explains the consequences of the catastrophic defeat. William Bullitt, U.S. Ambassador to France from 1936 to 1940, had steadfastly maintained in his communications to the State Department and to President Roosevelt that France was well prepared and able to hold off a German attack. He was not alone in that assessment and revisionist historians of the battle of France, such as Ernest May in his study, *Strange Victory* (New York: Hill and Wang, 2000), maintain that the French army had the capability to hold off Nazi Germany in 1940.

On July 3, 1940, a British naval squadron, after issuing an ultimatum to the French naval squadron to either set sail for British ports or scuttle itself, opened fire on French capital ships moored at Mers el-Kebir in Algeria, killing over twelve hundred French sailors and damaging several vessels. The attack by the former ally seriously damaged Britain's image with French public opinion driving many skeptical Frenchmen to rally in support of the new Vichy government. Virulent anti-British propaganda appeared immediately throughout occupied France in the form of posters, newspaper articles and editorials, pamphlets and books while the pro-German leanings of some members of the Pétain government were further reinforced. Some more extreme elements calling for war with Great Britain. But Hitler was not at all interested in a sudden rapprochement with an angry and defeated France and ordered Goebbels to discourage any such propaganda in Germany.[13] Nazi Germany had a completely different agenda.

The action at Mers el-Kebir came just as the French parliament, elected in 1936 when the Popular Front came to power, convened at Vichy. On July 10 the Assembly voted 569 to 80 to override the constitution of the Third Republic. Pierre Laval leveraged the British attack on the French fleet to push through a radical political change and successfully lobbied to have full powers granted to Marshal Pétain. New decrees were drafted and quickly signed by the Marshal creating the position of Head of State having far greater powers than any previous French leader, except possibly Napoleon. The personal prestige of Marshal Pétain was thought necessary to simply hold the country together as he was given the powers of an absolute monarch,

---

13. See Norman J. W. Goda, *Tomorrow the World. Hitler Northwest Africa and the Path Toward America* (College Station: Texas A&M, 1998), p. 20. The deep distrust Hitler and the Germans felt toward France and the Vichy regime was obvious from the beginning since it represented a potential threat to their long range plans. The Germans were convinced that Vichy was probably secretly pro-British in spite of all its public statements.

including the authority to amend the constitution and appoint his successor, in this instance Pierre Laval. The Third Republic and even the image of Marianne (the icon of the French Revolution) were soon replaced by the new name of "État Français" and the "Francisque," a double-edged hatchet in the shape of the Marshal's "bâton" became the symbol of its power. Technically, however, in spite of the vote of July 10, the Third Republic while suspended was never formally abolished.[14] In August 1944 Pierre Laval, following his instinct as the former elected member of a democratic parliament made an attempt to reinstate the old Third Republic assembly in Paris and even brought the reluctant former speaker Edouard Herriot out of prison to arrange for a possible transition. Laval was quickly rebuffed. The political foes he had persecuted in 1940 and who had been imprisoned and deported because of his policies were not about to help him. Laval was then forced to flee to Germany with the other diehards of the collaboration policy.

The new Vichy government faced a catastrophic situation: the French army had lost 126,000 dead to Germany's 97,000 killed in just six weeks of harsh fighting. There were over 1.8 million French officers and enlisted men being held as prisoners of war in camps or in transit to Germany. The army, navy, and air force had little or no fuel or ammunition left and was therefore unable to reach the closest French colonies in North Africa in significant numbers. The armistice provided that the French government would pay for the upkeep of the German army of occupation to the tune of 400 million French francs a day. But the government's most urgent task was to help the four

---

14. Maurice Martin du Gard in his *Chronique de Vichy* tells the following anec-dote: "The day Laval got the national Assembly to 'vote away' the Third Republic he said to Pétain: 'Well, Monsieur le Maréchal, are you satisfied with what I have got for you?' 'Yes,' said Pétain, 'it's perfect. But now Monsieur Laval,' he added after a short silence, 'you will have to learn to obey.' For a brief moment Laval thought it was a good joke and laughed." In Alexander Werth, *France 1940–1955* (New York: Beacon Press, 1966), p. 18.

million civilian refugees return to their homes, which in many cases were located in the "occupied zone," an excruciatingly difficult journey that required in each individual case the specific permission of the German military authorities.

According to the armistice agreement France was divided in two: the "occupied zone" north of the Loire River with Paris prolonged by an additional strip along the Atlantic coastline down to the Spanish border at Hendaye including the important port city of Bordeaux. The Vichy government exercised direct control over the southern "unoccupied zone" also known as the "zone libre." A majority of civilian public service employees, the "fonctionnaires," and the French military in the colonies chose to remain loyal to the Vichy government. Only French Equatorial Africa, except Gabon, joined General de Gaulle as early as August of 1940. The Germans viewed the defection as an ominous development since they wanted Vichy to retain control at least in the shorter term. In that same month of August General de Gaulle was condemned to death "in absentia" by a French military court.

Hitler and his staff never imagined that they would achieve such a fast and sweeping victory nor were they prepared to administer France and her colonial empire. On the contrary, the German high command was pressing to withdraw as many troops from France as it possibly could for the build up of "Operation Sea Lion," the invasion of Great Britain that was expected to take place during the summer. Hitler had signed off on the plan on July 16, 1940, but very quickly encountered logistical problems with the German navy that lacked the landing barges necessary for an amphibious assault. Admiral Raeder would soon ask for a postponement of the invasion to May 1941. At the same time, during the summer and early fall of 1940, Hitler was seriously contemplating "Operation Felix," a secret plan to attack and take the British fortress and harbor at Gibraltar thereby shutting the entrance to the Mediterranean and strangling the British Empire in the Middle East. There were indications at first that Franco's Spain was interested in concessions if it joined the Axis in the war. But the operation provided for the transit of German troops through Spain in order to attack the garrison at Gibraltar on land preferably with Spanish help. This required an agreement with General Franco who would progressively lose his enthusiasm as victory eluded Hitler and other Spanish generals voiced their opposition to actively joining the Axis.[15]

Both Italy and Spain made no mystery of their voracious territorial ambitions at the expense of the French colonies in North Africa: besides Savoy, Nice, and Corsica, Mussolini demanded Djibuti, Tunisia, a slice of eastern Algeria including Constantine, and more territory in Africa. By late June Spain had unilaterally occupied the international zone of Tangier, thereby replacing the French administrators and had its eyes on the rest of Morocco beyond the northern zone it already administered. Franco also wanted the western part of Algeria including Oran, and more territory further down the West African coast all the way to Senegal. But all these ambitions were in conflict with German plans for naval and air bases in Morocco and Dakar and the choice of Casablanca as the headquarters of the armistice commission in French Africa. Abwehr agents had been very active throughout French Northwest Africa for a long time.[16]

The most extreme French collaborators in Paris such as Marcel Déat and Jacques Doriot were vociferously demanding that France immediately join the Axis and the war but at that early stage Hitler and Mussolini were not encouraging such a move. The Germans preferred a quiet and submissive France that would eventually accept being amputated of large portions of its colonial empire. Whether this included full collaboration or

---

15. For British intrigues in Spain, see David Stafford, *Roosevelt and Churchill. Men of Secrets* (New York: Overlook, 2002).
16. See in greater detail N. Goda, op. cit.

not was indifferent to Hitler and most of the Nazi leadership. However the Germans were acutely aware of the dangers created by General de Gaulle and the Free French making a strong government at Vichy capable of enlisting the loyalty of the French people the preferred policy.

In the early fall of 1940 Hitler had good reason to feel optimistic about French collaboration regarding Gibraltar and North Africa. On September 23, 1940, a Free French and British naval expedition that included General de Gaulle, General Edward Spears, Churchill's personal representative now in charge of "handling" de Gaulle and the Free French, and Admiral Thierry d'Argenlieu, attempted to land at Dakar but was repulsed by the Vichy loyalist Governor Boisson and elements of the French navy. It was the first of several frustrating failures by the Free French to enlist more supporters in Africa further consolidating anti-British and anti-Gaullist sentiment among large segments of the population in occupied France and in the colonies. To many it seemed obvious that de Gaulle would soon be forgotten.

To launch his "Mediterranean" strategy Hitler suddenly decided to meet with General Franco at Hendaye on the Spanish-French border on October 23, 1940. Prior to taking the trip he held discussions with Mussolini asking him to keep his territorial demands in check pending a formal peace treaty at war's end. As Hitler's train crossed France it stopped for a surprise meeting with Deputy Prime Minister Pierre Laval on October 22 to prepare for a meeting between the Führer and Marshal Pétain. The purpose was to enlist the support of both Spain and France for the attack on Gibraltar, a German move into French Northwest Africa and the build up of Dakar as a major German air and naval base.

The meeting with General Franco was a fiasco from Hitler's point of view—Spain was starving and destroyed by four years of harsh civil war—and Franco, unsure of the loyalty his own generals despite his dictatorial powers, felt much too weak and uncertain to make any military commitments to the Axis. He told Hitler that Spain was in no condition to undertake any military operations and submitted a long list of requirements for food and supplies that clearly went far beyond what Germany could provide even if it agreed to do so. Nevertheless, still hoping that Franco would change his mind in the near future, on November 12 Hitler signed directive no. 18 or "Operation Felix," the attack on Gibraltar that would never take place. Later, in February 1941, Mussolini would make another attempt to persuade Franco but he was no more successful than the Führer and Spain never fully joined the Axis.

On October 24, 1940, at the small railroad station at Montoire near Tours, Hitler and Pétain shook hands for the newsreels in a highly dramatized sequence used by the French and German press to announce the policy of "collaboration" by the Vichy government. The Nazi leadership including Hitler was only mildly interested if not fundamentally hostile to any real collaboration with France at that point. The Germans viewed Laval as the best and most flexible political figure to deal with. He was the most accommodating and consistently eager to go beyond what the German authorities requested. In his friendly and folksy way, Laval also established close relations with Ambassador Otto Abetz, whose entire Nazi party career was based on cultivating Franco-German relations.

The failure of the Luftwaffe to bomb England into sub-mission in August and September forced Hitler to reconsider his options in North West Africa and the Middle East, the Balkans, and look to Russia, the biggest prize that had eluded Napoleon in 1812. France in that case would become a large supply base for workers, food and quality military hardware that French factories were able to produce. While collaboration, beyond the requirements of Germany's war machine, was of little interest to Berlin, the German embassy in Paris kept on encouraging the most extreme pro-Nazi sympathizers to do more for the Third Reich.

As Hitler looked east where, as he had written and preached in the past, Germany would at last find her "lebensraum," Nazi pseudo 'biological' and 'scientific' racial theories—inspired by his interpretation of Darwinian 'survival of the fittest'—also played a role in justifying his decisions.[17] France, according to *Mein Kampf*, was a bastardized country whose blood was hopelessly tainted by Jews, Blacks and other 'inferior' races. In France during the early stages of the occupation in 1940 the German military and the Abwehr were running things on a more or less exclusive basis while the SS, SD and Gestapo maintained a low profile only to become fully active much later in 1942, once the Wannsee Conference had set the stage for the Holocaust. Hard line French Fascists like Marcel Déat, Jean Luchaire, Jacques Doriot and others who were to play a more visible role in 1941 with the attack on the USSR, were sponsored and paid by Otto Abetz and the officers of the Propagandastaffel. Yet despite all this activity, according to Hitler's nightly monologues recorded in *Table Talk*, France remained Germany's "hereditary" enemy to the end of the war.[18]

The secret initial announcement of what would become the attack on the Soviet Union, "Operation Barbarossa" came on July 31, 1940, in the midst of all the commotion about Gibraltar and North Africa. Hitler rationalized to a group of generals among other things that to defeat England or convince her to come to terms with Nazi Germany he must first destroy Russia. He based his assessment that the USSR would be relatively easy

---

17. See Adolf Hitler, *Mein Kampf,* translation by R. Mannheim (Boston: Houghton Mifflin, 1938–2007) and Adolf Hitler, *Hitler's Second Book,* edited by Gerhard L. Weinberg (New York: Enigma Books, 2003).
18. "France remains hostile to us," said Hitler in one of his monologs on 31 January 1942, reflecting on the results of the collaboration policy, in H. R. Trevor-Roper, Ed., *Hitler's Table Talk* (New York, Enigma Books, 2000) p. 265.

to conquer following the purges that had destroyed the officer corps of the Red Army by Stalin in 1937–38, the poor showing of the Soviets against Finland in 1939–1940 and his conviction that he could knock the Soviet Union out in a five month spring and summer campaign in 1941. In November 1940 Hitler and Ribbentrop held meetings in Berlin with Soviet Foreign Minister Vyacheslav Molotov where strong disagreements surfaced as both Nazi Germany and the USSR were poised to compete over spheres of influence in the Balkans. Several historians believe, Nazi ideology and Hitler's planning notwithstanding, that the failed conference swept any remaining hesitation away and convinced Hitler that he must attack the Soviet Union as planned at the latest by the early spring of 1941.[19]

On June 23, 1940, the day the French armistice was signed, Hitler paid his second early morning visit to a conquered and virtually empty Paris, the first one having been on June 17, the day after the entrance of the German army. He spent time in silent meditation at Napoleon's tomb at the Invalides.[20] Later in the day he briefly attended the signing of the armistice at Compiègne in the clearing known as Rethondes where the railroad car used for the surrender of imperial Germany on November 11, 1918, had been symbolically rolled out once again for the occasion.

By the fall of 1940 the political picture seemed to be improving at Vichy. After Mers el-Kebir and Dakar most of the army and the colonies remained loyal to the government; the Montoire meetings with Hitler created a new atmosphere; the Germans grudgingly agreed to an accommodation with the new

---

19. See Gabriel Gorodetsky, *Grand Delusion. Stalin and the German Invasion of Russia* (New Haven: Yale, 1999). The "Operation Barbarossa" plan was delayed for six weeks in April and May 1941 when Germany diverted its forces to invade Yugoslavia and Greece, a move military historians see as the major cause for the failure to defeat the USSR during the first months of the invasion before the rainy season set in.
20. Hitler visited Paris twice: on June 17 and 23, 1940.

French regime meaning that they would not act on dividing the French colonial empire just yet. The United States, while refusing initially to acknowledge General de Gaulle's Free French as a legitimate government or even as a representative movement, preferred to entertain normal relations with Vichy much to the delight of Marshal Pétain and General Weygand. Admiral William Leahy, an old friend of FDR's from the First World War, was appointed U.S. envoy to Vichy France in November 1940. The Admiral was expected to arrive at his post in early January on what would be an important mission yielding very tangible results.

On October 28, 1940, Mussolini embarked on a disastrous rainy season campaign against Greece. Hitler was informed almost ex post facto and demanded an immediate meeting with Mussolini in Florence on the heels of Montoire. Italian troops became bogged down in the harsh mountains of Albania as the Greek army put up a strong and effective resistance to the invasion inflicting several defeats on the Italian army. The Italians were forced to retreat into Albania by November. That same month British aircraft taking off from an aircraft carrier staged a daring attack on Italian capital ships at the port of Taranto in what became a successful attack on naval forces from the air that was to inspire the Japanese attack on Pearl Harbor. In December British forces counterattacked from Egypt pushing the Italians into a five hundred kilometer retreat abandoning half of the Libyan coastline to El Agheila.[21] Those spectacular setbacks played a major role in deflecting any Italian pressure against France and its colonies.

Deputy Prime Minister Pierre Laval, a seasoned Third Republic politician, was of lower middle class origins, the bright son of an innkeeper in the town of Chateldon, in central France. He became a lawyer representing labor unions and was a socialist

---

21. See Gerhard L. Weinberg, *A World At Arms* (New York: Cambridge, 1994) pp. 210–211.

early in his career before the First World War. As his law practice grew, Laval moved to the conservative right but was never an extremist nor like many centrist French politicians, was he a Freemason although very much a part of the 'République des camarades' as the parliament of the Third Republic was known by its detractors. Laval, the quintessential pragmatic politician had mastered the art of the backroom deal and was convinced that as a good horse trader ("maquignon") he could hoodwink the Nazis with the same methods he used to get elected. To him the challenge was no different than being mayor and member of parliament from the working class suburb of Aubervilliers, north of Paris where he was regularly reelected by a large majority of a very left-wing electorate that enjoyed Laval's pragmatism and down home populist style. Laval had managed to become immensely wealthy as an investor in real estate and in various businesses; he owned several local newspapers to the point of actually being the richest politician in France at the time. His daughter Josée had married into French nobility to Count René de Chambrun, a direct descendant of the Marquis de Lafayette. Chambrun had been awarded dual American and French citizenship by FDR himself.

In the early fall of 1940 Laval was meeting regularly with the German top brass in Paris at the Hotel Matignon that he used as his residence—during the occupation the former palace of France's prime ministers was the only public building with central heating. He quickly appointed one of his loyal journalist friends, the aristocratic Marquis Fernand de Brinon, as his personal representative. Brinon was later given the bizarre rank of French ambassador to the German authorities in France. His counterpart was an old friend, Germany's ambassador to occupied France Otto Abetz, who was also residing in Paris rather than Vichy in a Byzantine arrangement.

Laval was conferring and making deals with Abetz and the German leadership without informing Pétain and other Vichy government officials, or at least not to their satisfaction. He was known to rarely take notes of his conversations or submit any written reports when he was foreign minister in 1934–35.[22] Laval, who had worked under Aristide Briand, was like his mentor essentially a negotiator, a man who used the spoken word as his preferred instrument of communication. The aging Marshal Pétain, found Laval vulgar and disrespectful, and resented his blowing thick cigarette smoke in his face when they would meet. The Head of State was soon voicing regret at having designated Laval as his successor. Pétain's immediate entourage also feared and resented Laval's power and the influence he had through his relations with the Germans while Laval made no mystery of his utter contempt for the old fashioned monarchists who were running things at Vichy.

The very first anti-Semitic measures at Vichy came quickly and almost went unnoticed: on July 17, 1940, a law restricting entry into the civil service to those having a French father was announced and enacted without much fanfare in effect barring Jews from government offices.[23] On September 27, 1940, German military authorities issued the first official anti-Jewish measures in the occupied zone calling for a large sign to be prominently displayed in the windows of all stores owned by Jews saying "Entreprise Juive."[24] On October 3, the German occupation authorities also required that all Jews apply at local police stations for a "census," warning that any attempt to disobey the order would be severely punished. Within weeks Vichy followed up with a more comprehensive anti-Semitic policy of its own thereby preempting any potential German demands.[25]

---

22. See J.-B. Duroselle, *France and the Nazi Threat,* (New York: Enigma Books, 2004).
23. M. R. Marrus and R. O. Paxton *Vichy France and the Jews* (New York: Basic Books, 1981), p. 4.
24. "Jewish Store."
25. "I have been unable to turn up any direct German order for French anti-Masonic, anti-Semitic or any other legislation during the most active period of

On October 18 the infamous "Statut des Juifs" was published in Vichy's *Journal Officiel*, detailing a set of stringent regulations preparatory to a more radical persecution of French and foreign Jews to come. Foreign Jews were often expelled by the Germans into the unoccupied zone and placed—in camps that had been previously used for Spanish Republican refugees—by Vichy authorities as early as November 1940.

The author of the "Statut des Juifs" was law professor and Minister of Justice Raphäel Alibert, a conservative admirer of Charles Maurras, who was determined to give a strong right-wing doctrinal imprint to the new regime. But Alibert would soon incur the personal displeasure of Marshal Pétain who would dismiss him in January 1941 and later complain that his former minister had provided him with "very poor advice." The anti-Jewish laws, however, continued to be enforced. Right-wing monarchist ideologues and traditional French anti-Semites, who were more xenophobic than racist in the Nazi mold, saw Vichy as a golden opportunity to create the kind of authoritarian system that would reverse the despised parliamentary and republican democracy. While Charles Maurras remained the strongest traditional right-wing ideological influence and continued to publish his daily newspaper, *L'Action Française,* in Lyon during the German occupation, he was never directly involved in Vichy policy making.[26] Maurras, a poet and "homme de lettres" from southern France was originally a follower of positivist philosopher Auguste Comte and felt more at home in the nineteenth than the twentieth century expressing a poetic nostalgia for the golden age of the French monarchy under Louis XIV. He became active in politics at the height of the Dreyfus case in 1899 taking an extreme right-wing position and using his trademark vitriolic prose to prove the culpability of Captain Dreyfus

---

Vichy legislation in 1940." Robert O. Paxton, *Vichy France Old Guard and New Order 1940–1944* (New York: Knopf, 1972), p. 143.

26 See Stephane Giocanti, *Maurras Le chaos et l'ordre* (Paris: Flammarion, 2007).

even when all the evidence pointed to the captain's innocence and continuing even after Dreyfus was rehabilitated. He launched a daily newspaper, *L'Action Française,* in 1908 and transformed his monarchist, anti-Semitic, and ultra nationalist ideas into a doctrine that he called "integral nationalism."[27] But, along with most French extreme nationalists, Maurras was also uncompromisingly anti-German and wanted above all for France to recover the provinces of Alsace-Lorraine she had lost to Germany in 1871. What distinguished Maurras from most other right-wing parties was the fact that his political movement, also called Action Française demanded the return of the monarchy and the end of the Third Republic. His strident anti-Semitism resurfaced when the Popular Front won the 1936 elections and Léon Blum became the first Jewish Prime Minister in French history. Maurras' articles were judged so violent that he was arrested for inciting to riot after Blum was attacked in the street and seriously injured by a group of student thugs. Maurras however was not held personally responsible and was eventually set free.

Maurras bitterly criticized the Third Republic governments and especially the Popular Front, which he wrongly accused of not adequately rearming France. In maintaining his old anti-German positions, he concluded that France was too weak and unprepared to go to war and became a right wing pacifist. In his daily columns he demanded an accommodation with Fascist Italy, supported Franco's Spain and strongly backed appeasement and the Munich agreements of September 1938. He saw Vichy as the ideal regime short of restoring the monarchy and

---

27. Prior to the Dreyfus Case there was a revival of French anti-Semitism after 1880 with the publication of the two-volume pamphlet by Edouard Drumont, *La France Juive.* Drumont was the editor of a newspaper, *La Libre Parole,* one of the most violently anti-Semitic sheets published in Paris at the time that certainly influenced Charles Maurras, Maurice Barrès and most of the Vichy anti-Semites. The books by Drumont were reprinted by the Paris publisher Flammarion in 1941.

mostly opposed Laval's pro-German policies: "Maurras claimed, indeed, for his press campaign the credit for having fully persuaded Pétain to get rid of Laval in the famous "palace revolution" of December 13, 1940."[28] There is enough evidence of how widespread the influence of Maurras was within France's upper middle class in 1938–1940 when many conservative officers, including Colonel Charles de Gaulle, were known to read his column daily even though they disagreed with his program. Maurras was the source of many if not most of the ideas incorporated into Vichy's "Révolution Nationale." The first Vichy of 1940–1942 was clearly a monarchist-leaning and Maurras-inspired regime.[29]

Marshal Pétain's entourage was filled with ardent disciples of Action Française who rejected the parliamentary tactics and the penchant for placing everyone in front of a "fait accompli" of the populist Pierre Laval. The main players in the story that follows acted according to their firmly held "Maurrassien" principles. When Laval returned to power in April 1942 and went to even greater extremes in collaboration, the ideas of Maurras were no longer the dominant ideology at Vichy. The Paris Fascist "collabos" were gaining ground and enjoyed the active support of the Nazis while the resistance was gathering strength and mobilizing in France.

Even though Marshal Pétain personally approved the decrees issued by his government, there is enough evidence to conclude that as victory eluded the Germans in Russia, he concluded that a liberated France would return to a parliamentary democratic and republican form of government. Pétain, like most Frenchmen, adopted a wait and see or "attentiste" attitude. As Georges Poisson shows, on highly sensitive and divisive issues Pétain exhibited indifference, especially regarding the fate of the Jews even though he was not known to have been per-

---

28. Alexander Werth, *France 1940–1955,* cit. pp. 71–72.
29. See Eugen Weber, *Action Française* (Stanford: Stanford UP, 1962).

sonally anti-Semitic and indeed had cultivated many important Jewish friends, nor did he share Maurras' position on the Jews before the war.[30] Pétain made sure his personal friends who were Jewish were spared the rigors of the anti-Semitic laws and in several cases helped them leave the country, on the other hand those Jews he did not know personally were of no interest to him. Laval was also known to have helped individual Jews through is son in law, Count de Chambrun.

In 1944 Laval was genuinely distressed to hear that Georges Mandel, who was Jewish, and a former conservative colleague in parliament as well as an important cabinet minister, had been assassinated in a cruel and cowardly manner by the Milice, the brutal special police force created by Vichy in 1943 to fight the Resistance.[31] Yet out of political expediency rather than anti-Semitism, like many Vichy politicians, Laval not only failed to oppose the most horrifying Nazi requests for deportations to the death camps but was actually accommodating adding to the numbers of those that were being deported to their deaths knowing that the heightened persecution of the Jews would

---

30. Charles Williams, *Pétain* (New York: Palgrave Macmillan, 2005). This excellent new biography shows how, as an officer during the Dreyfus Affair, Pétain did not voice any opinion or take sides in the debate about Captain Dreyfus' guilt or innocence and simply avoided the issue by keeping characteristically silent. Maurras' anti-Semitic position was that of an extreme xenophobic nationalist who considered that Jews as foreigners didn't "belong" in France and could therefore not become "Frenchmen." There was no pseudo-scientific justification comparable to the Nazis' "biological" theories but Maurras nevertheless applauded the "Statut des Juifs" and all the anti-Semitic measures taken by Vichy. Upon being told at his trial that he was condemned to life in prison, true to his old ideas he cried out "C'est la revanche de Dreyfus!" ("It's Dreyfus' revenge!")

31. Laval wrote in prison in 1945: "His death [of G. Mandel] was a great shock—all the more tragic because for a time I thought I had saved his life." Quoted in John M. Sherwood, *Georges Mandel and the Third Republic* (Stanford: Stanford U.P., 1970), p. 294. Mandel was murdered in a reprisal by the Milice following the execution of Philippe Henriot in Paris by the resistance on June 28, 1944.

make him much more acceptable to Hitler. But in 1940 those horrors had not yet taken place and very few imagined that Nazi Germany would engage in the massive genocide that became the Holocaust. Official German policy at the time was to expel the Jews from the greater Reich and relocate them in a country yet to be identified.

Marshal Philippe Pétain was 84 in 1940 when he became head of state. He was born in 1856 and belonged to the generation that had grown up under the Second Empire and had therefore seen two very different regimes rule France.[32] The son of peasants from the Pas-de-Calais department in northwestern France, he was raised by an uncle who was a priest and who helped the young boy get into a catholic boarding school. After some hesitation about the priesthood, Pétain decided to pursue a military career and eventually passed the entrance examination to St. Cyr. Throughout his life he would never be a religious man but consistently respected the Church and the Catholic clergy in particular. Prior to the First World War, Pétain had pursued an unremarkable but honorable military career where he was known to impose rigid discipline and exacting training on the young recruits under his command. The notable exception was the series of lectures on infantry tactics that he gave at the École de Guerre which impressed many other high ranking officers and helped get him promoted. In 1914 Pétain, already fifty-eight, was expecting to retire in two years when the war changed his plans.

During the First World War he rose quickly to the rank of general and practiced a very effective defensive and counter-attack strategy as a commander in the field. His strong leadership certainly ensured victory at the battle of Verdun in 1916. In 1917 he became known as the general who put down the mutinies in the trenches that almost paralyzed the French army while improving the lot of the foot soldier. In 1918 he was

---

32. See Charles Williams, *Pétain*, op. cit.

credited along with Foch, Haig, and Pershing as being one of the great military leaders who defeated the Kaiser's Germany. In December 1918 he was awarded the rank of Marshal of France for his service during the war, the highest rank in the French army.

By all accounts Pétain was a soldier's general who empathized with and understood the psychology of the "poilus" who fought bravely in the trenches and who came mostly from peasant stock similar to his own. Many of those who approached Pétain, such as General Edward Spears,[33] remembered him as a man of few well selected words and long silences, who was in the habit of writing short and terse reports. Pétain was very friendly with Spanish dictator General Primo de Rivera who ruled Spain from 1923 to 1930. He got along well with General Francisco Franco whom he met during the Rif campaign in northern Morocco in 1925 and whom he respected. In 1939 the French government appointed Pétain as its first ambassador to nationalist Spain. Contrary to later claims he never supported the extreme-right wing "Cagoule" in the late 1930s when a handful of French army officers were planning a coup d'état to overthrow the Republican regime. By his upbringing and temperament, Pétain was clearly politically conservative but he remained a cautious and mostly apolitical general who believed strongly in discipline and dedication to duty. Staging a military revolt was not something he would have considered no matter how much he disagreed with the government.

In June 1940 Pétain became Deputy Prime Minister in the government of Prime Minister Paul Reynaud. He reached the conclusion early on·that the war was lost and agreed with

---

33. General Sir Edward Spears was a British liaison officer in 1914 and later a Conservative M.P. He spoke fluent French and worked with most of the French superior officers in the First World War including Pétain whom he knew well. In May 1940 Churchill dispatched Spears as his personal representative to the French government. It was Spears who brought General de Gaulle to London from Bordeaux on June 16, 1940, in his aircraft.

General Weygand, the commander in chief of the French army, that the only solution was to negotiate an armistice with the Germans. On June 16 President of the Republic Albert Lebrun asked Pétain to form a government. The behind the scenes political maneuvers at Bordeaux were handled by Pierre Laval who was impatiently demanding an end to the war and busy making deals to get the new regime started. From the start there was merciless rivalry between the old Marshal and the politician. Laval had his group of followers in the political class while Pétain felt more at home with military men and the traditional conservatives close to the Action Française.

The rivalry and real antipathy between Laval and the men around the Marshal were bound to erupt given the negative articles published in Paris in the fall and winter of 1940 attacking Pétain's policies. The ultra collaborationists, and especially Marcel Déat, an eloquent philosophy professor and former socialist minister in 1935, who had started a new extreme right wing political movement, were demanding a one party system similar to that Nazi Germany and Fascist Italy.[34] Déat published a number of insulting articles in his newspaper *L'Œuvre* where he ridiculed the army, Marshal Pétain and the Vichy government in general. His writings annoyed Pétain who read them regularly and was told by his entourage that Déat was a creature of Laval.

In the fall of 1940 Adolf Hitler suddenly decided to return the ashes of the Duke of Reichstadt to France to be buried in a grandiose ceremony at the Invalides. The idea had been discussed before the war but it probably resurfaced when the Führer visited Napoleon's tomb in the Invalides rotunda in June 1940. Was it intended as a grand political gesture or just a form

---

34. M. Déat was one of the best public speakers in France in the 1930s and had even impressed Raymond Aron who wrote: "I must shamefully admit that much later I would be dazzled by the eloquence of Marcel Déat—very different from that of Paul-Boncour or Edouard Herriot, his was more factual, less emotional and enhanced by a tremendous speaking ability." Raymond Aron *Mémoires* (Paris: Julliard, 1983), p. 69.

of self-satisfying megalomania? Clearly Otto Abetz, who had championed the idea for years, saw it as a golden moment for both leaders, Hitler and Pétain, to meet once more for a memorial at Napoleon's tomb. Abetz dreamed of a very effective propaganda event that would convince even the most skeptical Frenchmen that Germany was the only country France could turn to in the new world order. A second handshake between the Marshal and the Führer at Napoleon's tomb would seal the policy of collaboration in the eyes of the world. Furthermore, the Marshal and his immediate entourage would best be accommodated at the Versailles Palace rather than in the cramped surroundings of the spa hotels in Vichy. The armistice terms specified that the French government would eventually return to Paris and this was the perfect opportunity to make that happen.

Nothing could have sparked the suspicion of the Vichy entourage of Marshal Pétain more than such a decision by Hitler announced by Laval that could radically alter the power structure in 1940. The men around the Marshal were convinced that Laval was in fact plotting a coup with the ultra collaborators in Paris and the Germans to neutralize the current leadership and bring Pétain to Versailles where a new and truly collaborationist and Fascist type regime would be set up. Pétain was therefore to become a powerless figurehead.

The only way to thwart those plans was to arrest Laval and even kill him if necessary. The plot was hatched on December 13 with Laval's forced resignation and arrest. His life was spared and he was kept under house arrest at his home a few kilometers from Vichy until Otto Abetz came running down from Paris to his rescue with a unit of heavily armed SS troopers.

The ashes of Napoleon II arrived in Paris in a somber and dignified cortege. Most observers understood that there was something strange in the fact that the casket was being escorted through Paris by German soldiers at midnight and that the next day only Admiral Darlan and a very angry Ambassador Abetz were on hand for the full dress ceremony. Marshal Pétain and Adolf Hitler were nowhere to be seen and the Vichy government would remain in its spa location in central France to the end in 1944.

American diplomats at Vichy applauded the firing and arrest of Laval and FDR and Cordell Hull were hoping that the French would adopt a more independent policy. The ashes of Napoleon II were returned to Paris, an unexpected and almost bizarre gift from the Führer, while the liberation of France was still four long and sad years away.

Robert L. Miller

Author's Preface

The history of the return of Napoleon's ashes in 1840 has been told more than once and I have also added my contribution a few years ago in a book that contains some unpublished documents. The success of that book encouraged me to research the story of another such return, that of the ashes of the Aiglon—the Eaglet, as Napoleon II was known affectionately to the French people—in 1940. It was a dramatic moment in the midst of defeat, an episode in stark contrast with the pomp and circumstance and the happiness of the earlier return of the father during the nineteenth century. Now the atmosphere was permeated by the gloom of the German occupation and the whim of a victorious dictator making an empty gesture. While the story itself had never been told, it was also the cause of a national crisis: the return of the body of Napoleon's son actually provoked the dismissal of Pierre Laval, the collaborationist prime minister, and for a brief moment everyone thought that there was still hope for France. It is interesting to recount those dramatic days that often had a tragicomic quality when one considers the characters involved: Pétain, Laval, Darlan, Brinon, Abetz… An unexpected turn of events unfolding in the gaudy surroundings of the Hotel du Parc at Vichy where Pierre Laval went from being the all-powerful heir apparent in the morning to being placed under arrest in the evening by the same policemen who had been loyal to him. It was to be Napoleon II's only victory, and a short-lived one at that, amid the many reversals in the life of the unhappy prince. He was returning to Paris only to experience how much he had been forgotten: there is not even a short alleyway bearing his name on the hill of Chaillot that had been landscaped in his honor, and his bronze casket remains invisible after resting for some sixty-eight years in the Invalides.

I was encouraged to undertake this work by Jean Tulard, Jacques Jourquin and others but I needed a publisher who was not exclusively specialized in the imperial period. My good friend Thierry Lenz the director of the Fondation Napoleon was well inspired to warmly recommend this manuscript to Nouveau Monde editions that is associated with the fondation but also publishes modern and contemporary history. That is how this book came into being. The author is very pleased and wishes to thank all those who kindly helped him in getting this work done besides the names already mentioned: Jean des Cas, Dr. Maurice Catinat, Thierry Choffat, René Deck, Michel Denieul, Jean-Mathieu Gosselin, Hon. Otto von Habsbourg, Mrs. Irissou also known as Monique Difrane, Jean-Claude Lachnitt, Jean Macé, Mrs. Anne Muratori-Philip, Mrs. Christiane Petillat, curator of the Centre des Archives contemporaines, Olivier de Rohan, Éric Roussel, Mrs. Oksana Willer-Garin, the historical service of the Defense ministry. I extend my gratitude to all those who will honor me with their reactions to this book.

Hitler's Gift to France

1.

The Crypt of the Capuchins

Sleep! But in your sleep dream what you
  Relived
And how by leaving your body in its copper
  Casket
I was able to steal your heart in its silver urn.

Edmond Rostand
The Capuchin's Crypt

"Let him wear his white uniform."

The well-known final repartee in *L'Aiglon* as imagined by Edmond Rostand with his unequaled feeling for theatrical drama had never sounded more real. On July 22, 1832, at the castle of Schoenbrunn where the window of his room opened on the "Gloriette" crowned with an eagle. The young man who had been crowned king of Rome and emperor of the French before being sacrificed to Europe's hatred and fear was reduced to the title of Duke of Reichstadt, and closed his thin lips. His embroidered nightshirt was removed and his already cold body revealed after an autopsy how the two most acclaimed physicians in Vienna had been completely mistaken for so many months about the prince's true ailments.[35] After removing his heart and insides he was dressed in his uniform of colonel of the Wasa Regiment with blue pants with silver embroideries, a white tunic with green ornaments, and the two decorations of the Austrian monarchy.

The room used for the wake is the exact same condition to this day. It had also been used by Napoleon; so that the father and the son had shared it some twenty years apart, with the same decorations by Franz van den Bercht with tapestries of Dutch pastoral scenes hanging behind a magnificent Japanese screen.[36] The "Eaglet's" body remained in the room on view on Sunday in all probability with very few guards on duty since his private possessions were stolen and his hair was almost entirely cut either by his entourage or an assortment of souvenir hunters.

On the following day the body was placed in the salon of Lacquers, wearing a hat and resting on a white cloth in an open casket on a table draped in black cloth. The crowd filed past all day through the Porcelains Cabinet where decorations climbed all the way up the walls, to look at the emaciated body with the sabre Bonaparte had worn in Egypt at its side to which the son was more attached than any other heirloom. The silently somber visitors then left through the Lacquers salon where a few remembered how Napoleon had lived and dreamed under the portraits of the emperors who had occupied it before and after him. It was there that, after the battle of Wagram, he decided to divorce Joséphine in the hope of perpetuating himself for

---

35. They were convinced the he had a liver disease like his father.
36. Upon returning to Schoenbrunn in May 1832 the prince couldn't go back to his usual rooms that were being refurbished. The Archduchess Sophie had lent him her rooms but he was moved to the first floor left wing so that he could have more sunlight in the same rooms Napoleon had used after the battles of Austerlitz and Wagram.

posterity. Now his only representative lay dead just a few steps away.

The castle refurbished by Maria Theresa in 1744 hadn't changed since that time: the father and the son saw it exactly as it has remained to this day.

During the night of the 23rd, the body carried by two lone horses and escorted by horsemen holding torches was taken from Schoenbrunn to the chapel of the Hofburg, draped in black and opened all day to all the Viennese who admired the courtesy and elegance of the young prince whom they always called, despite official orders, "little Napoléon." However glorious origins so loudly proclaimed were denied by the display next to the casket, of the ducal crown, the collar of Saint Stephen, since he had never been awarded the Golden Fleece, the military hat with the sword and belt of a superior officer. Dignitaries of the Austrian and Hungarian guard in their sparkling red and gold studded uniforms with a cocked hat or bearskin headdress were standing at the four corners. Priests were celebrating mass at every altar.

The body of the most romantic historical character of the nineteenth century could now be seen in a double casket (his father had been given five) on a representational bed framed by rows of candles. He appeared to be very tall and his face known to us thanks to Klein's sculpture had been ravaged by illness but since at the time no one had seen Napoleon's death mask and couldn't notice a likeness to be discovered later on.[37] On the steps was the prince's coat of arms: leopards and chimeras had replaced the "N" and golden bees.

Two hours later the heart of the deceased was taken by a chamberlain in a silver urn to the chapel of Loreto of the church

---

37. The beautiful sculpture is on display at Schoenbrunn castle. A reproduction would be fitting at the church of the Dôme of the Invalides if only to remind visitors that the prince's casket cannot be seen today. (See the Epilog.)

of the Augustines, the castle's chapel near the tomb of Leopold II, while his insides placed in a copper vase went by a coach with glass windows to the vault of Saint Stephen cathedral. Those sad remains have not left their resting place since that time.[38]

At five in the afternoon the double casket was placed into a heavy bronze molded sarcophagus decorated with lions heads with huge rings in their mouths on its sides. It was then placed on a funeral chariot covered in red Moroccan leather, pulled by six white horses, and escorted by a double line of soldiers from the Wasa Regiment. The court followed in parade carriages to the sound of a rolling drumbeat. Passing through the Josephplatz, the convoy reached the Neue Markt, in front of the door of the church of the Capuchins selected by the emperor Mathias and empress Ann because of its austere appearance, as the mausoleum of the Habsburgs. Crown Prince Ferdinand the uncle of the dead prince welcomed the casket into the church along with all the archdukes who were present in Vienna. A new church service was held inside and after a final absolution the sarcophagus was lowered into the crypt where Czernin, the grand master of the Court, had to answer the ritual questionnaire:

"Who goes there?" asked the father superior.

"I am Franz Duke of Reichstadt of the Habsbourg race," answered Czernin for the dead man.

"I don't know who he is. Who is asking to enter here?"

"I am the grandson of His Majesty the Emperor of Austria."

"I don't know who he is. Who is asking to enter here?"

Czernin then dropped to his knees.

---

38. The tradition of separating in three different locations the remains of the Austrian imperial family began in the seventeenth century since this scattering underlined the vanity of life on earth and to multiply the locations of the remains of the deceased to increase the number of pilgrims. Today after a refurbishing the silver urn containing the Eaglet's heart is in the crypt of Loredo and can be recognized at its small tricolor ribbon. The entrails remain under the main altar of the cathedral of Saint Stephen.

"I am Franz, a poor sinner and I implore for God's mercy."

"Then you may enter."

Once the casket was in one of the lower rooms the Franzensgruft, according to tradition, Czernin had it reopened to show the body to the priest as the guardian of the crypt. Since that moment no one has ever again seen the face of the Eaglet. The sarcophagus was locked with two keys; one was given to the prior and the other was taken to the imperial Treasury.

The original crypt of the church had been the burial ground of the Habsburgs since 1633 but Empress Maria-Theresa had the French architect Nicolas Jadot built a vast round crypt called the Kaisersgruft for a spectacular tomb that Napoleon visited accompanied by monks carrying torches. Inside that Habsbourg version of Saint-Denis,[39] in nine separate rooms where the heavy bronze caskets were stored in a dusty disorder, some on a pedestal and others simply lay on the ground. This was the case for the Aiglon's sarcophagus with a Latin inscription restoring him after twenty-eight years to his true identity and illustrious ancestry:

"In the eternal memory of Joseph-Charles-Francis Duke of Reichstadt, son of Napoleon, Emperor of the French, and of Maria-Louisa, Archduchess of Austria, born in Paris on March 30, 1811. Saluted at birth as the King of Rome; at the height of his mental and physical powers and in the flower of youth, of a tall bearing, handsome face and particularly graceful speech; remarkable through his aptitude for military service; having fallen ill with tuberculosis—he was taken by the saddest death at the imperial palace of Schoenbrunn near Vienna on July 22, 1832."

The imperial court went into mourning for six weeks. The prince's casket was placed facing that of Maria-Theresa. Three years later his grand father the Emperor Francis II who had been

---

39. The Abbey of Saint-Denis to the north of Paris is the burial place of all the French Kings. [NDT]

defeated at Austerlitz and Wagram was placed next to him surrounded by his four wives in a heavy and much higher sarcophagus.[40] They were to remain there for over a century. Among the visitors, the French looked at the long casket of Napoleon's son, and a few of them would bring bouquets of violets.

Apart from the occasional visits of tourists, the memory of the young man buried in the crypt of the Capuchins faded quickly. When King Louis-Philippe decided in 1840 to send for the remains of the Emperor Napoleon at Saint-Helena and bury them under the dôme of the Invalides there was no thought of doing the same for his son, whom a few older Parisians remembered seeing for the last time in March 1814 in the uniform of the National Guard at a review at the Carroussel while the palace intended for him was being built on the hill of Chaillot but quickly interrupted.[41] To the King of the barricades—Louis-Philippe—the solemn return of the ghost of the man who had ruled Europe was akin to playing with fire as the future was to confirm. To request the return of the son who had died only eight years before and whose uncles and cousins were still alive would have represented political folly and no one even brought it up.

However as soon as Napoleon III came to power he asked that Austria return the body of his first cousin but Franz-Joseph steadfastly refused to do so. Was it the counsel of the old Metternich who remained hostile to the young man who had died twenty years earlier? Or was it because of the rumors circulating in Vienna that the emperor's mother, Archduchess

---

40. The casket of Marie-Louise placed next to her son in 1847 is now with Maximilian in the Neue Gruft built in 1960.

41. We point out that in order to build that palace by architects Percier and Fontaine, the Emperor cleared the hill of Chaillot of its houses and gardens that later allowed for the construction of the palaces that were to follow. It was originally for the King of Rome that the area changed so drastically but there is no street or even an alley that bears his name.

Sophie had loved the Duke of Reichstadt, and as shown in various photographs as she holds two small boys on her knees, Franz-Joseph and his brother Maximilian, and that the Eaglet was thought to be the father of the latter? Without any allusion to these unlikely rumors the Viennese court answered the Tuileries that in its opinion the deceased was, and remained what he was intended to be, that is a Habsbourg.

2.

Hoping for a Return

As the years went by the Austrian dynasty was increasingly beset by tragedy. Following the Duke of Reichstadt, the crypt of the Capuchins witnessed the arrival of Maximilian, executed by firing squad in Mexico in 1867, of Rudolph who died at Mayerling and was probably murdered in 1889,[42] of the Empress Elizabeth murdered on Lake Geneva in 1898, and of the Archduke Francis Ferdinand killed at Sarajevo in 1914, the first to die in the war that took millions of lives. Franz-Joseph finally entered in 1916 overcome by age, family tragedy, and defeat.[43]

---

42. See Jean des Cars *Rodolphe et les secrets de Mayerling* (Paris, 2004).

43. The emperor ended the tradition of the dispersal of the remains. His father, the Archduke Francis Charles who died in 1878, was the last Habsbourg to be subjected to the custom. Since the burial of Empress Zita in 1989 the crypt includes some 130 bodies of imperial family members.

The Austro-Hungarian Empire collapsed two years later and France as a victorious nation could have easily made the return of the Aiglon part of the treaty of Saint-German. It would be too simple to say that no one thought of it, the Quai d'Orsay diplomats were in charge of such matters. Perhaps Clemenceau in his visceral hatred of the Habsburgs ruled out the idea. Public opinion in any case was not made aware of it.

In 1930, two years before the centennial of the Aiglon's death, the issue was first raised and a movement in favor of the return began that included Prince Murat as well as republican politicians like Anatole de Monzie and Paul Painlevé. A committee was formed directed by Edouard Driault president of the Napoleon Institute,[44] where Prince Murat was a prime mover, to commemorate the Aiglon's death and promote the idea of the return of his ashes. A solemn mass took place at the Invalides. The return of the body had elicited thousands of signatures but required the agreement of the Austrian imperial family who still controlled the crypt of the Capuchins. Baron de Bourgoing went with General Koechlin-Schwartz who was the representative of Prince Napoleon in France—since by law he was still forced to live in exile—to the castle of Steenokkerzeel near Brussels. The Empress Zita and her son the Archduke Otto received the two delegates and amiably listened to their request; as owner of the crypt the archduke promised to agree if the request came officially from the French government. The magazine *L'Illustration,* which was always very patriotic, immediately commissioned one of its writers, Albéric Cahuet, the author of the novel *Pontcarral,*[45] to publish for the centennial, a long study of the Aiglon and how his remains could be returned to France. However historian Octave Aubry, in his book *Le Roi de Rome,* published in 1932, remained skeptical:

---

44. He was the author of a book entitled *Le Roi de Rome.*
45. *Pontcarral* was a popular patriotic and very Bonapartist novel. He published an article 'Le centenaire de la mort de L'Aiglon,' *L'Illustration,* July 22, 1932.

"His return would be too understated. Where would his remains be placed? In the Invalides? Everything there is arranged so that Caesar can sleep alone surrounded by the Victories. This new casket at his feet would be less inspiring than if it were to remain a prisoner..."

Within the committee there were differing opinions as to the location of the casket once it was returned. Others proposed, perhaps to ensure that the Aiglon would continue to be viewed as a victim rather than an actor, that he be placed at the palace built for him at Rambouillet with a few buildings left as they are seen today.[46] But the majority was in favor of the Dôme of the Invalides without saying exactly where he would go because space was already in short supply.

"When I returned," recalled Koechlin-Schwartz, "I immediately spoke to Foreign Minister Édouard Herriot who approved the project and set the date of December 15, 1940, as the moment of the return of the ashes." A tragic future was to ensure that such a date would be kept. "The minister even decided that the ashes of the Aiglon would arrive at the Invalides railroad station." Said the general, "and would be taken under the dôme with the full military honors due to a Grand Cross of the Legion of Honor."

But this was no time to set the rules, and some opposition did appear, in particular that of Joseph Paul-Boncour who was probably hoping to inject some substance into his desperately empty political career. The government soon fell and the project was quickly shelved. Napoleon's name still frightened too many people in France.

A new attempt came immediately following the Munich crisis. On November 7, 1938, counselor Von Rath at the German embassy in Paris was shot dead by a young Jew, Herschel Grynzpan. The incident received a lot of attention in

---

46. Paluel-Marmont, "A propos du retour de l'Aiglon," *L'Illustration*, December 21, 1940.

France and especially in Germany where it became the cause of
the Kristallnacht on November 8, 1938. However a small group
of French utopians who made up the membership of the
"Association France-Allemagne" through its spokesman
Fernand de Brinon whom we shall meet again later on, felt that
the Nazi regime having at last reached its goals, however
unpalatable they may have been, meant that reasonably friendly
relations were again possible. Prime Minister Neville Chamberlain had proclaimed "Peace in our time" after all immediately
following his return from Munich. A few young right-wing
French intellectuals who had recently discovered Nazi Germany
among them Robert Brasillach, the future collaborationist
journalist, wrote unambiguously that: "They had more or less
slept with Germany and that it had been a pleasant feeling." The
French government appeared to share this kind of wishful
thinking and invited Nazi Foreign Minister Joachim von
Ribbentrop to Paris for a bilateral declaration, known as the
Bonnet-Ribbentrop agreements that were signed on December
5, 1938. It was on that occasion that an odd individual who was
destined to play a leading role during the period of collaboration,
suddenly appeared on the scene.

Jacques Benoist-Méchin was thirty-seven at the time, an
ambitious somewhat aloof,, handsome man, who was very
careful to hide his homosexuality and was also very anti-
Semitic.[47] Among other things his interests ran to music, translation, journalism and right-wing politics at the Association
France-Allemagne but he was best known as the author of a
multi volume history of the German army since 1918 published
to great acclaim in 1938. It was a monumental work that De
Gaulle admired. History in his case was practically a family
matter: his ancestor was Alexandre-Edme Méchin who as a
prefect under Napoleon, was awarded the title of baron of the

---

47. Jacques Benoist-Méchin was wounded in 1918 during the bombing of the
church of Saint-Gervais.

Empire on December 31, 1809, and there were rumors that Mrs. Méchin had been the Emperor's mistress.[48]

Without acknowledging it naturally, the young man didn't object to being called "baron" Méchin, a title he had no legal right to bear because his ancestral ties to the prefect came only through women. Marie-Elizabeth Méchin (1832–1873) had married Alfred Benoist, a tax collector, and their direct descendant Stanislas Lucien Benoist had obtained by a decree dated June 27, 1879, the authorization to bear the ancestral name which didn't necessarily imply that he also had the right to the title. Was it because of this Napoleonic ancestry of sorts that the young man thought of proposing once again the return of the Aiglon's ashes?

Benoist-Méchin was invited to give a lecture in Berlin on November 10, 1938, on the subject of the French and German armies and was summoned by Ribbentrop to the Wilhelmstrasse the next day as the German foreign minister was preparing his upcoming trip to Paris to sign a number of agreements. The German foreign minister was asking about the kind of welcome he might expect from the French public. Benoist-Méchin attempted to explain that the recent aggressive actions by Germany (the Rhineland, Austria, and Czechoslovakia) had all managed to create a climate of great hostility in Paris. Ribbentrop then stated that the Reich was not at all hostile toward France and his visitor who, according to Eric Roussel, "was an intellectual lost in the political arena" came up with a spectacular suggestion.

"When a guest is unable to extend an invitation in return he can always send a bouquet of flowers, a gift of sorts…"

"What kind of gift would you see me offering to France. I don't see anything…"

---

48. See Jean Tulard, *Napoléon et la noblesse d'Empire* (Paris 2003), p. 282. On his mother's side J. Benoist-Méchin was also related to the famous surgeon Larrey.

"Yes, your Excellency, there is something you could give. And should you do it quickly enough, I am sure your visit to Paris will take place in a very friendly atmosphere..."

"What do you mean exactly?"

"Return the King of Rome's remains to us...You cannot imagine how popular the historical figure of the Aiglon still is in France! He is the stuff of legend. Give us back his casket so that we may place it in the Invalides next to his father. The gesture will touch the heart of every Frenchman and will give your visit..."

The foreign minister did not let Benoist-Méchin finish the sentence:

"I am afraid I cannot consider your request. I don't see the point. It would be a purely sentimental gesture without any political significance..."

Benoist-Méchin later explained:

"I did my best. Mr. von Ribbentrop simply had nothing to offer."

Upon leaving the Wilhelmstrasse the Frenchman went to pay a visit to Otto Abetz who was in charge of Franco-German relations and whose office was close by. Abetz is also fated to play an important part throughout this story.

Born in the Rhineland, Abetz at the time was a rather large and tall man of thirty-five, who had worked in France as an art teacher and was well connected to cultural circles in Paris.[49] He was known for having organized meetings and events between war veterans of both France and Germany and had worked toward reconciliation between the two counties. He even made a proposal to have two unknown soldiers, one French and the other German, buried side by side in the cathedral at Strasbourg. Abetz had married a French woman and was completely bilingual; he possessed extensive knowledge of French literature

---

49. Blond with blue eyes, he had a very German need to be liked that outdid his equally Teutonic desire to dominate.

and pretended to be much more of a Francophile than he actually was. He had joined the Nazi Party and the SS in 1935 and was heavily involved in promoting Nazi propaganda as a member of the "Ribbentrop Office." All these activities led the authorities to order him to leave France in 1939.

Benoist-Méchin quickly became friendly with Otto Abetz who showed great interest when he heard the Aiglon story seeing how it could serve his purpose and further his career. He asked Benoist-Méchin how the project could actually work. The visiting Frenchman with his customary enthusiasm and creativity suggested that two committees be set up, one German and the other French to include well known personalities and descendants of historical figures from the Napoleonic era. The German committee was to withdraw the casket from the crypt of the Capuchins and take it solemnly to the middle bridge at Kehl where it would be handed over to the French committee that would in turn, convey it to the Invalides.

Abetz's reaction was enthusiastic and he commissioned Benoist-Méchin to form the French committee and promised to have information about the German committee before his return to Paris. When he called four days later the matter had acquired a life of its own.

"I took the liberty of presenting the idea to the Führer.[50] He thought it is an excellent idea and said: "So Benoist-Méchin had that idea! Why hasn't Goebbels thought about it before? That's his job!"

He immediately called Arthur Seyss-Inquart the Gauleiter of Austria to get things started and then Joseph Goebbels to make a number of rather unpleasant observations. At the same moment Goebbels was meeting with General Pariani, the head

---

50. It sounds surprising that Abetz, who at the time was a minor civil servant of the Wilhelmstrasse, would go directly to Hitler over his boss Ribbentrop's head. Perhaps Benoit-Méchin embellished the story as he was often prone to do.

of the Italian militia, with whom he shared in the strictest confidence the dressing down he had just been given. Pariani in turn was indignant: to return the son of the Corsican, a province that Italy was claiming as its own, the son that Napoleon had dared name King of Rome! Mussolini would phone Hitler shortly after that this would be seen as an unfriendly gesture quite contrary to the spirit of the Axis.

Hitler was however fascinated by the possibility and wanted to see the project succeed even more since so many people were trying to thwart it.

"This is why he asked me to tell you that if it cannot happen at present he will hold on to it in any case and will promote it again as soon as circumstances will allow," Abetz told Benoist-Méchin.

We may assume from then on what the intentions of the two men were: Benoist-Méchin wanted the return of the Aiglon's ashes as a conciliatory gesture by Germany intended to erase at least the bad sentiments of the past two years.

He was hoping that Munich was the final crisis of that kind. To Hitler, who never had any friendly disposition or intentions toward France, it was just another step in his dream to equal and surpass the conquests of Napoleon, a figure that haunted him just as much as Charlemagne had haunted Napoleon. Hitler wanted to emulate the charisma and persuasive energy of Napoleon who had also shown an unlimited appetite for acquiring more land. France had wanted the return of the ashes of Napoleon in 1840 so therefore Germany would be promoting the return of the ashes of the Duke of Reichstadt in 1940.

Benoist-Méchin requested written confirmation of the project and its status something Abetz agreed to do. He published the letter that also contained a very Nazi sounding paragraph:

"There is a beautiful symbol in the fact that the cradle that belonged to the King of Rome shall remain in Vienna, which is his mother's homeland while the casket would go to Paris to rest next to his father. The son having been close to his mother in childhood will be with his father in his work and in death."

The project would not be discussed any further but Hitler didn't forget it. On December 6 Ribbentrop signed the agreement in the Salon de l'Horloge at the Quai d'Orsay, where the atmosphere was formal and unusually cold. A visit to the Invalides was on the itinerary but the German foreign minister cancelled it and returned home "disappointed and flustered" as Benoist-Méchin commented. The advocate of Franco-German understanding couldn't accept to see that policy remain unfulfilled. Hitler was intent on pursuing his policies of annexation, which the French government felt compelled to oppose.

The Daladier government lost interest in the Aiglon if it had ever truly considered it while Benoist-Méchin's initiatives and his German friendships only managed to attract the attention of the Deuxième Bureau[51] that kept on harassing him after he was drafted during the "phony war." He decided to endure that kind of treatment avoiding any appeals to Marshal Pétain who knew Benoist-Méchin since he was a child and who addressed him in the familiar form: they were destined to come into close contact soon enough.[52]

Less than twenty months after Ribbentrop's visit to Paris Hitler, after his victory in the battle of France, visited Paris twice on the 17th and 23rd of June, 1940. On the second occasion he landed at Le Bourget airport and in the company of architect Albert Speer and the sculptor Arno Breker, the official artist of the Nazi regime, who was often compared to Michelangelo but he didn't even come close to the Italian artist. They drove in a large convertible Mercedes for an early morning tour of the

---

51. French military counter espionage. [NDT.]
52. According to Marcel Déat in his *Mémoires politiques,* who on this and other issues is not very reliable. Déat was writing in exile many years after the fact and often embellished the past.

deserted French capital. Breker described the visit to the Invalides: "following a detailed survey of Hardouin-Mansart's masterpiece we went inside. It was impossible to not be affected by the solemn atmosphere inside…Hitler was holding his cap pressed against his chest. He bowed in the midst of an imposing and solemn silence…We were expecting Hitler to find words that would measure up to the place and the moment. Then something totally unexpected happened: he spoke of the Duke of Reichstadt, Napoleon's son whose remains were buried in Vienna. He declared that the return of the ashes would be a magnificent gesture that could be the sign of a reconciliation with the French people and he ordered that the remains of the Duke of Reichstadt be transferred to Paris and placed next to his father."[53]

Hitler viewed this as his revenge against those who had thwarted his desire originating from his passion for Napoleon rather than any real inclination to please the French people.[54] It was intended even less, as some writers have speculated in 2005, to use Napoleon to condone the massacre of the Jews. Of course it was impossible for the project to get started immediately but it was set in motion as of August as soon as Otto Abetz was appointed ambassador to Paris. The preparations took place in the greatest secrecy and were hidden from both Italian and French authorities—Hitler's unexpected decision set in motion the dramatic story that follows.

---

53. Arno Breker was loudly celebrated as a great talent during the occupation with a large exhibit in Paris and was later to be criticized before finding his true dimension. The exhibit's catalog had a preface by the great sculptor Charles Despian, who was later attacked because of it. ("He placed himself in a 'Breker' situation. [A play on words for "précaire" or precarious, which sounds like "Breker" – NDT.] The attacks hastened his death in 1948. I went to his funeral and it was poorly attended.")

54. "France, the mortal enemy of our nation…." Adolf Hitler, *Mein Kampf* (Boston: Houghton Mifflin, 1943), p. 666. One wonders whether the officials at Vichy read those words?

3.

The Making of a Palace Revolt

"Early on, as a child, Pierre Laval felt and thought of himself as someone who was disliked by other people."

Jean-Paul Cointet, *Pierre Laval*

Hitler's visit to the Invalides came at the start of those first six months when France was attempting to survive amid its ruins. It was just before July 3, 1940 when the French navy was bombarded and sunk because of the terrible mistake and indeed the crime perpetrated by the British at Mers-el-Kébir which was made even worse because of the blunders of Admiral Gensoul. On July 10, 1940 the National Assembly met at the Vichy Casino under the influence and manipulations of Pierre

Laval who orchestrated[55] the voting of constitutional powers to Marshal Pétain[56] who was proclaimed "head of the "État Français.""[57] The government set up its offices on July 1 at the Hôtel du Parc one of the best in the city of Vichy, a large building commissioned by the Swiss hôtelier Aletti with a corner dome over three streets but that was usually closed in the winter since it had no central heating. A number of coal burning stoves with their stovepipes jutting from the windows had to be installed. In contrast to that slum look the lobby quickly took on the military atmosphere where the old soldier felt at home now that he was the supreme leader of the nation. The Marshal's Guards were formed as of November 1940 (no French head of state had had a personal guard since the end of the Second Empire in 1870) that was made up of gendarmes over 5'10" with leather helmets, white gloves and blue pants with black stripes. They were experts at parade evolutions and the changing of the guard became a popular spectacle similar to that of the palace guard at Monaco and they presented their arms when the head of state appeared. On Sundays the flag was raised with pomp and circumstance and the ceremony was presided over by Marshal Pétain, often in uniform with his seven stars on his sleeves, wearing his military medals and képi with three rows of

---

55. On June 23 Pierre Laval was appointed Minister of State and on June 27 Vice President of the Council of Ministers. His power of persuasion insured his success at the National Assembly while his last executive post as Prime Minister from June 1935 to January 1936 had not been successful and his deflationary policies it turned out worsened the financial crisis.

56. Pétain and Laval had first met in 1931 during an official visit to the United States for a commemoration of the war of Independence. They had both served as ministers in the Doumergue government and became closer when Josée Laval married René de Chambrun son of an old army comrade of Pétain.

57. It was rumored that Pétain had decided on that name replacing the President of the Republic to force everyone to address him as "Monsieur le maréchal" since one could not say "Monsieur le chef." The way the decision of the National Assembly was to be interpreted and used after July 10, 1940, was for all intents and purposes a real coup d'état.

oak leaves; his mustache perfectly trimmed.[58] But he never wore the red sash even when he received newly accredited ambassadors nor did he display the marshal's star studded bâton. Pétain waxed sarcastic about German marshals like Göring or Keitel who liked to brandish that emblem. He often liked to use rough barracks-type speech and would address his male listeners:

"I always wear my bâton on me especially in the morning. But I don't show it to just anyone..."[59]

In the company of his wife, after the ceremony Pétain, who did not believe in God and had married a divorcee, went to mass at the Saint-Louis church, a rather mediocre pseudo-Gothic building commissioned by Napoleon III with stained glass windows representing Saint Napoleon, Saint Eugénie, and Saint Horteuse. Pétain actually enjoyed more the accoutrements of power to its reality: he enjoyed being seen.

The Marshal chose to live on the third floor of the hotel in just three rooms that he found adequate. He was used to living in hotels and kept his trunk packed and ready under his brass bed. He was served by military orderlies and only by men who were not picked by his wife "Nini" whose chatter often bothered her husband who made sure she was quartered in the Hotel Majestic located across the street.

Every morning and in all kinds of weather the Marshal would go out in his civilian clothes with his homburg, his cane and flower in his lapel, for a constitutional walk in one of Vichy's many parks.[60] If it was raining he would opt for the eight

---

58. It (the mustache) "had the impeccable whiteness that goes with virtue," wrote René Benjamin.

59. Pétain never liked ceremonial attire. He was the only marshal without a formal uniform with black dolman and plumed "bicorne" (perhaps because of his stinginess) and unlike Foch and Lyautey he never ordered an academician's uniform. As head of State he never once wore the grand collar of the Legion of Honor that had a medallion with his name engraved on it.

60. The "Parc des Sources" was created by decree by Napoleon while he was in Russia in 1812.

hundred meter passageway made of cast iron materials from the 1900 Machine Exhibit that he had visited at the time. Straight and erect, he answered the well-wishers, teased the children, often stopped for a chat with a veteran but didn't like to mix in larger crowds. There was no danger of his running into beggars, newspaper vendors, or undesirables who had all been banned before the war.

Pierre Laval, the Deputy Prime Minister and the Marshal's designated successor, had his offices on the second floor; where Gobelins tapestries covered the walls.[61] Laval usually known for wearing a fedora and striped suits was in the habit of letting the ashes of his cigarettes drop on his trademark white ties that Prime Minister Aristide Briand had suggested he wear to distinguish himself more. He would keep his white tie fastened all the way to the firing squad.

Laval had a deep love of his country and was not personally corrupt. He was also undoubtedly one of France's most intelligent political leaders, a rare example in a political class that had few men of his caliber active at the time even though there were many more politicians than half a century earlier.[62] His greatest handicap was a belief in his own superiority while he was actually lacking in many areas. He enjoyed and excelled at back room deal making while he also used to his own benefit in other areas such as farming and real estate and naturally in parliament. However, he failed to exercise caution and insight in foreign affairs where he encountered several major failures in 1935 with the USSR and with Italy. His immense self-confidence

---

61. There was nothing in the law voted by the National Assembly authorizing the Marshal to decide such a momentous constitutional issue. Without making any changes, the Marshal quickly regretted having appointed Laval. As he told Paul Baudoin: "If the Germans give me enough time I'll go back on my decision to name him as my successor."

62. J. P. Cointet studied Laval's finances at length. He did become a rich man through his profession and speculation but never appears to have used his political influence to do so.

ended up turning him away from the republican parliamentary democracy he was identified with and into becoming the enemy of all political parties in imitation of Mussolini. Laval was sincerely convinced of being right in every instance. Without any regard for the condition of subjugation France was living under, he would mindlessly tackle any problem head on rather than attempting to avoid it. He was used to barter as though it were a game and gambled that he could always come out on top.

At the Hotel du Parc, foreign affairs were located on the ground floor and the first floor. A few among the more privileged ministers had managed to secure small living quarters on the fourth floor, which under the preceding regime of the Third Republic would never even have been considered for a second class administrator and where their wives managed to cook as best they could on a hot plate against the hotel's rules and regulations.

To the Marshal, as the successor of Napoleon, this temporary location in a spa was a lot like being exiled on the island of Elba; but became a place from where he would never be able to escape that was more akin to Saint Helena. Perhaps he would have been better off dying at Vichy just as his illustrious predecessor had done on his far away little island.

It was in that ornate resort hotel with its gaudy furniture that Pétain would on his own initiative be the first marshal of France to launch a revolution.[63] Without waiting for the war to end he would at the outset attempt a "social and intellectual resurgence," a new order called the "National Revolution" forgetting that both Mussolini and later Hitler had used that very same terminology when they started out.

---

63. On August 19, 1941, Pétain told the Council of State (the equivalent of the US Supreme Court), "The irresistible forces of circumstance more than the wishes of individuals and even less my own placed me at the head of the State."

During the first few weeks, the Vichy government even managed to successfully reject new German demands over Morocco. Deputy Premier Laval was traveling regularly to Paris for discussions with the Germans and with Abetz in particular who was quickly becoming heftier both physically and politically. He was able to make his greatest wish come true when he secured his own appointment as German ambassador to Paris with Achenbach, an arrogant Nazi true believer, as his deputy. Abetz remained rather skeptical and polite by comparison.[64]

Laval had wanted that promotion. He had known Otto Abetz for a long time, ever since he had staked his career on a Franco-German understanding that would naturally benefit his native country. Less of a Francophile than he pretended to be, Abetz according to J. P. Cointret "Had toward France the love lust of a Pygmalion for his pupil." He distrusted Vichy's "National Revolution" almost as much as Laval who often shrugged his shoulders upon hearing that slogan. Using his established friendship with the new ambassador, Laval, who never had and never would understand the first thing about Nazism, was very much wedded to his tried and true political habits. He was convinced that he had played the right card and of being infallible as he attempted to improve or bypass the terms of the armistice often by making painful concessions. There included the outrageous costs of paying for the German occupation troops (400 million francs a day) and the de facto annexation of Alsace-Lorraine which was contrary to the

---

64. "They say he is very much the hedonist but is also naïvely pleased to show off at the embassy with a beautiful French woman of the Flemish type, a former secretary of Jean Luchaire. She likes royal lilies and dresses with elegance. She was a good wife and mother, something that mattered little to German career diplomats who barely acknowledged the fact that she not be German but were very critical of the fact that she had once worked as a secretary." Maurice Martin du Gard

armistice clauses and that Laval refused to put up a fight for.[65] As Darlan was to say: "He was one of those statesmen whose deep convictions were so strong that they obscured their view of reality and who once they had embraced an idea or a project are ready to make any concession as long as it came to fruition."[66]

Haunted by the thought of reaching a peace settlement with Germany before she defeated England (the German bombing campaign had begun on August 8) and therefore to secure a position for France, Laval was trying his best "to be nice" as he would say toward German occupation officials without seeking Marshal Pétain's opinion or even keeping him informed. Even though he was only deputy premier he acted as though he were the prime minister providing the chief of state and his staff with "vague and messy" reports (R. Cole.) One of Laval's mistakes was to have regarded Pétain as a figurehead. As Henri Michel writes:

"Laval neither reads nor writes reports. He hails from the school of Briand: speaking is his way of working. Pétain who was experiencing memory loss and was hard of hearing had trouble in following Laval's verbal improvisations that fluctuated up until the end of a sentence, and were also filled with digressions, asides, and anecdotes. He quickly got lost among those meanderings and later had trouble remembering them. Pétain was convinced that his vice president was seeking to confuse him or was hiding important matters."

And the Marshal was probably right.

"Who does he think I am?" he muttered, as he felt hurt more in his ego that in reality. Who was it that France had called upon, Laval or myself?

---

65. As Prime Minister in 1935, Laval had facilitated the return of the Saar to Germany.
66. Quoted by Alain Darlan, *L'Amiral Darlan parle* (Paris: Amiot-Dumont, 1953).

For Marshal Pétain, Laval's greatest shortcoming was to think of himself as being indispensable. He kept the habits of the Third Republic and viewed in Pétain a sovereign who did not govern, therefore giving him succinct oral reports when the old and rather deaf soldier expected concise reports on paper. Laval held his colleagues in the government in contempt: "a bunch of hair-splitters" as he called them.[67]

He was convinced that England was either already defeated or about to be. Yet Paul Morand who returned from London in August 1940 offered Laval some useful advice that he, Morand, wouldn't take: "If the Germans have not landed with the high tides then they will never invade England." By September 15 Hitler had lost his advantage. But Laval didn't believe it and was obsessed by the thought of overtaking Italy for second place behind a victorious Germany. Convinced of his cunning (J. P. Cointet explains it as "the fastest and safest way to reach his goals"), of his ability to "swindle" his opponents, he was forever self-assured:

"Let me swim on my own. I'll take care of the Boche!"

We may shrug off that kind of dark self-possession but not deny Laval a kind of unabashed sincerity.[68]

He harbored illusions not just about his own qualities but also about the enemy's intentions. Hitler's policy was clear: while seeking to broaden the advantages of his victory he also needed to foster a spirit of resignation and blindness among the French people. He had to make sure the French accepted the state of servitude they had been plunged into and even take part in it so

---

67. "If instead of closing himself so completely, President Laval in November and December 1940 had agreed to think things through, to discuss and debate issues with his colleagues, things would have been different." Yves Bouthillier, 1949 in *La Vie de la France sous l'Occupation* (Hoover Institution, Paris, Plon 1957).
68. Far from being able to master events as he thought he could in his proud naïveté, events were to lead him on and crush him in a kind of fateful ending reminiscent of Aeschylus." Marcel Peyrouton.

that the west would remain relatively peaceful thus allowing Germany to prepare its offensive in the East. That was the mission of Otto Abetz who happened to be particularly well suited for the job since he was both patriotic and a Francophile. One of the masterful cards to play to advance his policies was precisely the return of the Aiglon, an idea that was very much on Hitler's mind.

At the same time, unknown to anyone at Vichy, a few individuals were again working on such a return. In September 1940 Félicien Faillet, the editor of the magazine *L'Illustration*[69] in the course of a conversation with German officials mentioned the project of the return of the Aiglon and requested that this be done on December 15, the anniversary of the great return of Napoleon.[70] It is possible that his suggestion may have possibly been relayed to higher authority.

No one at Vichy was discussing the Duke of Reichstadt but more and more under Laval's prodding, the talk was about the possibility of a collaborationist policy that was requested, if not begged for by Vichy.[71] The policy was symbolically enacted on October 24 with Pétain's meeting with Hitler at the railroad station at Montoire that set the stage down an irreversible path. It was clearly a gaffe that settled nothing, offered no tangible results for France but that did have vast psychological implica-

---

69. I happen to remember Félicien Faillet—son of the poet Fagus—editor of *L'Illustration* and a man of great quality. The magazine was viewed as having collaborated because of two of its writers who had been imposed by the Germans. Jacques de Lesdain and Robert de Beauplan. *L'Illustration* was shut down in 1944 and Faillet sentenced to several years in prison and expelled from the Legion of Honor. Sixty years later it must be said that the punishment was unjust.

70. Robert de Beauplan, "Le retour de l'Aiglon en France" in *L'Illustration* December 21, 1940.

71. As J. P. Azéma writes: "Contrary to the widely repeated legend, Germany never demanded that France collaborate and only wanted her to be submissive and available to plunder." Hitler had barely acquiesced to the policy of collaboration. See Henri Michel, *Vichy, année quarante*, 1966.

tions. The handshake between the victor and the vanquished, and Marshal Pétain's statement announcing the collaboration policy had a negative effect on occupied France: "One of our country's most serious misunderstandings," according to Robert Aron.

At the first cabinet meeting on October 26, after Montoire, Laval stated: "Abetz hopes to see French and German soldiers fighting side by side one day. That's his dream. He wants to be liked. Those are very good and friendly feelings." Those words elicited some rather sharp reactions: René Belin worried that France would some day be fighting the British and Pétain immediately injected that would never happen. After some four months of armistice many felt that it was necessary "to sound the alarm and take a position against German high handedness and Italian aggression," as Admiral Fernet said rather naïvely by comparison to Laval's cunning.

Montoire, which Pétain compared exaggeratedly to Tilsit, did nothing to improve Franco-German relations. The only small concession came on prisoner of war issues and Pétain used the opportunity to have his faithful friend General Laure freed to walk the corridors of the Hotel du Parc "with his empty skull" as Marcel Déat wrote, reduced to the role of aide de camp. However at the court of Louis XIV the most lowly tasks were in fact assigned to the highest aristocracy.[72]

"One had to be either stupidly cynical or incurably naïve to take Hitler's promises seriously. Unfortunately for the country Vichy combined both of those mistakes as J. P. Azéma writes. Improvements in the occupation regulations were still expected but not only did they not come to pass, but the armistice agreement was constantly being broken, bypassed or subject to interpretation by the Germans. The plundering not only continued

---

72. Arrested by the Gestapo in 1943 General Laure was deported and later tried and acquitted in 1948. General de Gaulle eulogized him at his death in 1957.

but after November 11—the Germans having an odd conception of the importance of anniversaries—whole train-loads of French citizens living of Alsace and Lorraine who had been turned out of their land began arriving. The German Reich had actually always viewed the offer of an agreement with disdain: the only true believers in collaboration were Laval and Abetz. The latter would later write with the lucid vision of those who stand defeated: "Rather than the massive freeing of prisoners of war and an easier crossing of the demarcation line, a reduction of occupation levies and the administrative return of the northern departments, the only thing France obtained following the solemn policy declarations at Montoire were the trains filled with citizens being deported from Lorraine." Montoire was not at all as some have written, a diplomatic Verdun but rather a Canossa. Abetz would send a report to Ribbentrop on November 19 that would transform what was called collaboration into what amounted to the German colonization of France.[73]

In the six weeks from Montoire to the return of the ashes of the Aiglon, the policy of the Vichy government appears divided into increasingly opposed tendencies. Pierre Laval, the natural born debater, who believed in the power of words, the back room negotiator and horse-trader, known as the "Talleyrand of Aubervilliers" was convinced that Montoire was his international success story.[74] "With the Germans you have to become a rug merchant." Laval treated Pétain as a symbol; he felt "sincerely that he was the real leader of France as though he had inherited a crown as the successor of thirty generations of Kings" wrote Yves Bouthillier. He was spending as much time in Paris as in Vichy and followed his own policy completely oblivious of the official representative in occupied France General Fornel de la Laurencie, a handsome and rather unsophisticated military man

---

73. See Henri Amouroux, *Pour en finir avec Vichy,* vol. II, Paris, 2005, p. 375.
74. *La Vie de la France sous l'Occupation,* op. cit., p. 1610.

with offices in the rue de Grenelle, in what used to be the ministry of Labor where he had posted two municipal guards wearing sabers. Laval was also increasingly using the services of a former journalist Fernand de Brinon.

Brinon was a strange character. A true aristocrat, exceedingly "well bred," an excellent speaker, always eager to be of service, Brinon was not very dependable where money was concerned. Before the war he had become a trusted follower of Adolf Hitler ready to take any path the Führer chose. Brinon was therefore destined to become one of the most hated men in France and yet during the entire occupation period he also managed to save hundreds of prisoners who were being sentenced for racial or patriotic motives. He believed in a German victory until the very last moment and even tried to keep a fictitious French government allied with Nazi Germany alive to the end. At his trial Brinon would not allow that his lawyers plead his case for clemency in the High Court as though he wished to underscore the hopelessness of his position.

Physically he had a large hooked nose that was the subject of more than one joke and several anti-Semitic rumors. He had married Lisette Franck, who was Jewish but had been "aryanized," and had a reputation as being an incorrigible gossip. She was known as "la marquise." The couple was not a happy one.

The politicians referred to him as "Brinontrop." Laval, ignoring General La Laurencie, had designated Brinon as his personal representative in the occupied zone. The marquis was to work as hard as he could to secure an agreement with the Nazi regime that expected to remain in power for one thousand years.

The "swarthy Auvergnat" Laval, simply shrugged off the increasing hostility on the part of other government ministers. Just like Napoleon with Talleyrand, he would repeat the unlucky words of the Duke de Guise "They wouldn't dare. They know—

he would say with his trademark self assurance—what I will manage to obtain from the Germans. If I must I'll pound the table and they will scatter like rabbits into their warren. I shall save the country in spite of them, all of them!"

It was a strange mix of willpower and naïveté.

Laval continued to bargain, attempting to gain some advantages to France during his meetings with Otto Abetz, in exchange for the loudly proclaimed collaboration policy by making new and disastrous concessions (ceding the Bor mines and the Belgian gold). As Weygand would tell him to his face in his clipped and disdainful voice "You revel in defeat like a dog rolling in his own shit." But nevertheless the man from Châteldon persisted in charging forward convinced that would manage to hoodwink the Germans as he had managed to do so effectively before the war with other politicians thereby improving or even reestablishing France's position without skimping on the concessions he had to make or worrying about the support of the French people. Laval showed no interest in the opinion of the head of state, the only person among his peers that he didn't find it necessary to convince and he remained oblivious or even dismissive about the old warlord's capability to maneuver.

As Julian Jackson writes: "In spite of his reputation as a cynic, Laval was an extraordinarily naïve man. He made the mistake of overestimating the importance of Abetz who had less influence over German policy than he thought and than the interested party hoped." Favoring in principle, as in the past, an understanding between the two countries, the ambassador was ready to attempt to loosen his grip but he never forgot that France was the defeated enemy. Whether he was responsible for it or not, France had gained no advantage, and Germany remained obstinate in its refusal about the point in the armistice agreement regarding moving the government to Versailles. The point was discussed for six months in fruitless meetings and the issue was also tied directly in December 1940 to the return of the ashes of the Aiglon.

Pétain, on the other hand, wasn't too enthusiastic about "Mr. Laval's collaborations," that in Laval's mind were meant to improve the daily living conditions of the French people. But he had obtained no results prompting the Marshal to blame his deputy prime minister for that failure. On the other hand, Pétain understood as of October that the British had won the Battle of Britain in the air and that they wouldn't be invaded. He was also convinced that it was necessary to negotiate with them.

But Pétain, whom most Frenchmen considered to be a healer able to cure every ailment that plagued them, had a grand design in creating new institutions. These were inspired by an old fashioned, conventional nationalism inspired somewhat by Charles Maurras, and even more by André Tardieu and the policies of Salazar in Portugal. The National Revolution was a hope for some, a revenge for others, and a diversion for those with a wait and see attitude. As André Siegfried wrote it was: "The explosion of century-old repressed disagreements, hatreds and dashed ambitions." It was essentially traditionalist anti-democratic, pathologically nostalgic, clerical, backward looking, paternalistic, placed under the symbols of virtue and the energy of a few perennially praised writers like Charles Péguy and Henri de Montherlant, friendly to the army (in spite of the defeat in 1940), to agriculture, and to the labors of artisans. Vichy was characterized by a rather simplistic and primal spirit of reform, crystallized into a naïve philosophy of the state. The whole thing was packaged in an anachronistic bundle, defended by Pétain and his faithful followers with "a kind of confidence and satisfaction bordering on pure arrogance" as S. Vergez-Chaignon wrote. Laval dismissed the entire matter as the pet project of an old man: the revolution was a reaction. The result of this wave of conservatism was a massive number of dismissals for a variety of reasons during a moment of "White Terror."[75] All this without even mentioning the fact that being Jewish, was viewed as a major crime in the Vichy government—the armistice agreement never mentioned the issue at all.[76] The Marshal became the focus of a personality cult unparalleled since Napoleon, which was actually much more spontaneous. A multitude of posters, postcards, pictures of all kinds, brochures, children's books even, that used every possible technique to place the image of the head of state everywhere, along with the famous words "I give myself to France" that in the final analysis meant very little. This wild cult that, as early as the fall of 1940, appeared in the form of postage stamps, and busts of the Marshal that little by little would replace those of the Republic, symbolized by the sensuous Marianne, in France's municipal buildings, as J. P. Cointet has written: "the Republic had disappeared by omission." Street names were changed to Marshal Pétain and the symbolic "Francisque" was molded into coins.

The campaign was replete with hagiography and exaggerated praise, the most telling example being writer René Benjamin who was the most ridiculous by far:

"He [the Marshal] represents the daily honest effort at the end of which he saves us in the transparency of a dispassionate soul. When you think about it, it brings tears of happiness to one's eyes."

Even Napoleon had never ordered that kind of official glorification and did not entirely accept it. The Marshal took advantage of his naturally majestic looks and did not interfere with this propaganda when he didn't actually encourage it. He

---

75. The senior positions that were suddenly opened were given paradoxically to top naval officers who were being recycled into jobs they knew little or nothing about. The joke going around was of an "Admiral's Protection Association."

76. As the first anti-Jewish measures were made public General Mordacq who had worked for Clemenceau went to visit Pétain: "Marshal, you are dishonoring our uniform." "I don't give a damn," he answered.

was also increasingly worried about the actions of his deputy prime minister for whom he felt a physical repugnance.[77] The good-looking military man instinctively despised the ugly "Auvergnat" Laval. Pétain quickly began hating an individual he disliked intensely: he was vulgar, blowing the smoke of those endless cigarettes directly into his face. Laval easily smoked two to three packs of Balto a day, which yellowed his fingers and darkened his teeth. He was often unkempt and failed to show the Marshal the courtesy the older man came to expect. Pétain thought of his deputy prime minister as the caricature and the symbol of the kind of Member of Parliament that he hated most. Pétain would have accepted an upper class bourgeois, with good manners, who was ready to defer to the head of State, someone like Tardieu, Flandin or Monzie. Of Laval, Pétain would repeat with the stubbornness of old age: "That man is betraying me. I don't want him around anymore."

U.S. diplomat H. Freeman Matthews would write: "I heard Pétain too many times speaking of Laval as "that dirty little Auvergnat" not to be convinced that his antagonism ran deep." Laval actually had a very swarthy complexion that made him look unkempt rather than dirty. There was also the military hero's suspicion of a man who hadn't gone to war and was exempted from military service because of varicose veins...The Pétain-Laval duo was clearly mismatched.

The shadow of the Aiglon prompted both the physical and intellectual antipathy that Pétain felt toward Laval.

At times the "old man," as some dared refer to the Marshal, who enjoyed having guests for lunch and dinner at a well-appointed table, would then allow his ill-feelings to surface. This happened even more once he stopped having his meals in the hotel dining room, where he was barely separated from the last

---

77. As Yves Bouthillier commented: "He never shed a kind of vulgarity of his socialist beginnings that shocked the Marshal. There was a fundamental and permanent incompatibility."

tourists by a screen. Later on Pétain used a private dining room where he was served on plates and silverware adorned with the double-headed axe. Even the chandelier had the shape of the Vichy "Francisque." The artifact was unfortunately disposed of later on...[78]

Pétain had to manage on his soldier's salary all his life and was now happy to enjoy the comforts of a head of state with a civil list, which he had the authority to increase at will. Lunch in the dining room—rather than dinner time at the end of the day once the fatigue of old age would take over—was the Marshal's moment of triumph. A poor debater, he had trouble holding his own in a political discussion that he generally avoided and preferred a kind of gossipy light-hearted banter. Surrounded by pretty women when they were invited, he would tell jokes, recount old stories—often repeated—as he made pleasant remarks. He was unable to entertain at receptions at that time but the lunches represented his very personal form of "court" that was the opposite of Louis XVI who almost never allowed anyone at his table.[79] Pétain invited people easily and most of the time extended the invitation to all those visiting him, or to any important guests traveling through Vichy. His ministers were often seen at his table, especially Raphael Alibert who had been the inspiration behind the whole regime. Pétain was concerned as to the quality of the menus despite the restrictions of those years. He wouldn't hesitate to invite those who came to see him as adversaries, and perhaps he thought like Laval, that he would manage to charm his enemies. In this he rarely succeeded. When he was at Vichy, Laval only rarely made an appearance at the Marshal's table and preferred to have lunch at a restaurant near

---

78. Actually the historical Frankish axe rarely had two edges and certainly no tricolor decorations or the Marshal's bâton.
79. Pétain had also accepted responsibility for the debts of his son-in-law Pierre de Hérain, ambassador to Madrid. The Marshal was very demanding regarding the entertainment budget which he found ridiculously low.

his office. Pétain noted that on a rare occasion when Laval was invited, he would remove the crust from the cheese in order and eat it after he had finished the inner paste.

As J. P. Cointret writes, "Pierre Laval, known to everyone as the most ardent collaborator, was out of step with Vichy as far as internal politics were concerned." and he would often take a position against his own colleagues in exchanges such as the following:

"All members of parliament are crooks," said General Maxime Weygand.

"All military men are dumb," answered Laval.

The other ministers would comment about Laval with some apprehension:

"What new surprises will he bring back from Paris?"

The Vichy ministers ganged up against their colleague and deputy prime minister who kept everything to himself and was privileged to possess the only permanent travel document issued by German authorities allowing him to cross the demarcation line at will. Laval's Vichy enemies concluded that the Montoire declaration had only caused more problems, additional duties and humiliations for France, and that it turned out to be the complete opposite of any form of "high level policy."

The top Vichy ministers were to play a key role in the tragedy set off by the Aiglon's return and the main characters in the unfolding drama deserve portraits of their own.

Yves Bouthillier came from the Charente region and specifically the island of Ré. He attended the École Centrale, was a government financial specialist and had been practically retired by the Popular Front. Paul Reynaud brought him back as finance minister which represented an exceptional promotion at the time for a top civil servant. He remained as minister under Pétain, when he had to deal on a daily basis with the gigantic financial withdrawals that the Germans were demanding. Any one of Laval's concessions turned into a budgetary problem. "The issue," he dared say on November 10 to Marshal Pétain in his clipped manner of the high level governmental manager, "is to see whether it is you or Mr. Laval who shall have to leave his post."[80]

His colleague Marcel Peyrouton, the minister of the interior, felt the same way. Peyrouton had been a Resident General in Tunisia and Morocco and later ambassador to Argentina from where he returned wearing belted overcoats and crocodile shoes. He had a reputation for being an energetic administrator, was much more colorful than Bouthillier, as a dynamic, active and often brutal man prone to making many faux pas.[81] It was said that he fired people left and right and never promoted anyone, which as Laval would say, made many people unhappy on the same job!

Paul Baudoin had attended the École Polytechnique and was the typical elegant and aloof upper class Frenchman. He was Vichy's first foreign minister.[82] He appeared to have a convoluted mind and was, as Maurice Martin du Gard would write in his chronicle, "a bit effeminate, always in the know, and very sharp. He had all the attributes to please the Marshal who happened to like him at that point in time. I am careful to mention "at that point" because with Pétain one never lasted too

---

80. Bouthillier would be arrested by the Gestapo in 1944 and deported to Germany but after being liberated he was still condemned to serve three years in prison in 1947. He died in 1977 after having been elected mayor of Saint-Martin de Ré, his home town.

81. Peyrouton's father-in-law was Louis Malvy who had earned a bad reputation a politician. As a Freemason he left the fraternity under Vichy—although it had greatly enhanced his career. Also retired by the Popular Front he had been brought back by Paul Reynaud who appointed him to be resident general in Tunisia. On September 6, 1940, he replaced Adrien Marquet as minister of the interior. When he showed some hesitation in taking the job, Pétain said coldly: "Just follow orders. If they told me to do the dishes tomorrow I would certainly do it. Now go back and sit in your chair."

82. It was Paul Reynaud's mistress Countess Hélène de Portes who had lobbied to place him in the government.

long." Laval, on the other hand, despised the tall and handsome Baudoin of whom he was probably jealous. He made sure Baudoin didn't attend the meeting at Montoire, thus provoking permanent hatred on his part. Laval then grabbed his job and transferred him laterally to a secondary ministerial appointment.

Raphaël Alibert, a big and very talkative law professor, was the jurist of the first Vichy group. He was both a convinced monarchist (who knows, therefore, what he really thought of the Aiglon), as well as an unabashed megalomaniac who could be almost dysfunctional. His colleagues nicknamed him "Fufurax" (or the "very crazy one") after a successful radio play of those years.

Laval would explain:

"The Marshal was being counseled by all kinds of weird characters who were all as adept at politics as I would be as the recruiter for Barnum and Bailey circus clowns."

Pétain would meet with his ministers in a tight little room on the ground floor of the hotel around two tables placed side by side in a totally different atmosphere than that of the Third Republic. There was no discussion of any points in the agenda or even any form of disagreement, the Council had all been decided in advance. The Marshal who was a bit deaf would ask each one to explain an issue and offer a solution that the head of state would either approve or disapprove. Twenty years later General de Gaulle was to use more or less the same method, but he never would engage in any of Pétain's barracks type humor: "slowly the railroads are improving. When the station master is present, everything works" said the minister of transportation. Pétain would cut in: "And suppose the station master is a cuckold?"

In November Bouthillier was back on the warpath against Laval speaking for all those who agreed with him as he told Marshal Pétain: "The danger is equally acute for you as well as for us and the future of our government action." And after all

King Louis XVIII who had also been forced to obey the occupying power had been able to rid himself of two of his prime ministers: Talleyrand in 1814 and Fouché in 1815...

As usual one minister had yet to voice his opinion. It was the Admiral of the Fleet Jean François Darlan. The sailor from Gascony was vain and rather vulgar—as Lehideux would say, "he is incapable of saying 'shit' in a distinguished way." The admiral was not a man of culture and was of rather average intelligence but he possessed a burning ambition. Darlan was dreaming of being another Admiral Horthy even though the Hungarian would be remembered as having betrayed his king. Darlan, however, knew how to navigate in spite of being called a "desk admiral"—he was expert at avoiding problems and pitfalls, carefully studying the winds of the storm that would knock down Laval. Darlan still thought that Germany was going to win but he was not about to help her do so and kept his wait and see position that remained anti-Laval but would eventually change.

The resolve of this often doubtful and timorous group was encouraged by another financial expert, Henri du Moulin de la Barthète who had met Pétain in Spain. The Marshal "was always favorably impressed by tall, well groomed men of character who were capable of making a decision, who had a good memory, which he lacked, and could express themselves in a clipped and synthetic manner that he was constantly seeking." as M. Martin du Gard wrote. Lucien Rebatet was more pointed in his assessment: "A rather handsome man with dark eyes, barrel-chested and filled with arrogant upper-class self-importance." Marshal Pétain also felt that this disciple of Charles Maurras talked "too high, too loud and too much." He added to the Vichy intrigue that would unravel on December 15, the date of the Aiglon's return "that could never have even been hatched had facts not created the event" as R. Tournoux put it. And as Albert Mallet wrote: "Laval of course was well informed of the way the wind was blowing and began thinking that Pétain needed to be set free of his entourage." That opportunity was soon to be at hand.

By the end of November the pace of events began gain momentum. On the 29th, in the company of de Brinon who had been appointed to the rank of ambassador to Paris, Laval held a meeting at the Hôtel Matignon with the ministers of war and marine, General Huntziger and Admiral Darlan to receive specific demands by the Germans.[83] French sailors were to attack British ports in Gambia and Sierra Leone; a French offensive was to be carried out against the colonies—Chad, Cameroon, the French Congo—that had joined de Gaulle. Chad was the most important because the RAF was refueling its planes in Fort-Lamy to carry out operations against the Italians in Libya. Should that operation become impossible, France was at least expected to bomb Bathurst, Freetown, and Fort-Lamy. Abetz was to write in his report that Laval had been singing his praise for "the magnanimous gesture, a unique event in history" of the Reich chancellor by offering collaboration to France and expecting her to become part of a European coalition against England. As Tournoux would write: "There wasn't a verbal expression that was deemed too slavish by Laval. He viewed words as having value only for a brief instant, you used them then tossed them in the dust bin of history." Laval forgot however that he couldn't address the occupying power in his country with the same vocabulary as his precincts at election time. He agreed to the German demands with his usual mental restrictions.

Typically Darlan had said nothing during the Franco-German meeting: Huntziger dragging his feet brought up

---

83 This would be the only time in French history that a French government had sent an ambassador to Paris, of all places. De Brinon was appointed Ambassador of France on November 4, 1940.

practical problems but Brinon felt as the meeting ended that they were heading toward co-belligerency with Germany.[84]

At Vichy the news gave rise to a renewed offensive against Laval and the cabinet meeting held on December 2 in his absence rejected the entire agreement of November 29 and heard an anti-Laval indictment by Bouthillier who proceeded to reveal the matter of the Belgian gold. His colleagues who were either indignant or devastated were still hesitating as to what they should do next.

Bouthillier talked about handing in his resignation. At the end of the cabinet meeting Pétain took him aside: "Don't you leave, he will be the one to go!"

The anti-Laval group used the occasion of a trip by the head of state to Marseille.[85] The Marshal was given a warm welcome, with many marches and patriotic songs to get him ready to carry out the still hypothetical firing of the man Weygand called "the Marshal's evil genius." On the way back at the railroad station at Avignon, the "dapper old gentleman," an expression that the newspapers were asked to avoid, saw a rather thin young man among the officials and looking at him with his steely blue eyes.

"And who do you represent, my friend?"

"The press, Marshal."

"Who is your boss?"

"President Laval."

"I will not compliment you about that."

Pétain made sure that everyone heard his words and understood that Laval was as unpopular as he, Pétain, was popular and that his firing would be viewed positively by the public.

---

84. Josée Laval later would say that her father, wanting to remain coherent with his pro-German policy, had agreed without intending to carry it out. *La vie de la France sous l'Occupation,* op. cit. p. 1655.

85. The official automobile column in Marseille went by a crowd of working class citizens. A young girl said out loud, "Oh! Does he look handsome!" When Peyrouton turned around she went on: "Not you, asshole!"

Darlan, who knew that Pétain quickly became intellectually tired and that he had trouble accepting any new idea, was beginning to understand which way the wind was blowing.[86] On December 4 in Toulon the Admiral confided in Bouthillier: "Old friend, just give me a sign and I will march all the way..."

Like Laval he was still convinced that Germany would win the war but also thought another outcome was possible.

Henri Amouroux wrote about the "conspiracy of a group of second raters." This author would rather state that they took their responsibilities seriously and deliberately. Only a sudden and totally unexpected event such as the return of the Aiglon could move them to action.

On the same day a secret message from Foreign Secretary Lord Halifax came where he cautiously accepted the principle of a limited agreement between Vichy and London. Despite Pétain's latent hostility toward England he agreed to the offer of suspending the British naval blockade and the promise not to attack the breakaway colonies. He felt tied to this dotted line agreement that the British wouldn't take seriously. This complete disagreement with Laval's ideas led the Marshal to accelerate his dismissal.[87]

---

86 Many statements have been made about Marshal Pétain's intermittent senility and his orderly Captain Bonhomme would say, "He is a very, very old man. His thoughts are no longer connected to action." At certain hours of the day one could see the drop in his intellectual acumen, those blank moments that René Benjamin described: "For a few minutes the Marshal retreats into the back of his mind, in some secret conversations." (Le Grand Homme Seul.) But often Pétain was aware and used those "absences" of his just as he used the fact of being hard of hearing to his advantage. "Between the crises he may doze off, whether literally or not. Once the alarm rings he rises to the occasion. He understands the information, the contradictory advice goes from one to the other and then returns to his own balanced center and the original positions: he stays with his men and defends them." Pierre Almeras.

87. Pétain was still resentful of the British for denying him the supreme command in 1918 and the sinking of the French fleet at Mers el-Kébir on July 3, 1940, didn't help at all. On the other hand he was very well disposed toward the Americans whom he liked.

On December 9, the head of state was comforted in his decision by the visit of General La Laurencie, a good but somewhat naïve soldier. He brought with him a file on Marcel Déat that he left with the Marshal.

Déat was a stout little man with a thin mustache, a philosophy professor who had been a government minister during the Third Republic and was elected to the National Assembly from a Paris district. Déat had broken with the Socialist Party and taken an uncompromisingly pacifist attitude with his provocative article entitled: "To die for Danzig?" As R. Tournoux would write he "turned from socialist red to nazi brown." The armistice then made him an extreme collaborationist, as he demanded a "one-party system," a formula he would dream about for four years and that was expressed in his unrelenting hatred for the "wait and see" groups at Vichy. "Thinking mostly in abstract terms, he was incapable of any kind of doubt either about himself or regarding any other politician." in the words of M. Martin du Gard. Actually Marcel Déat who claimed to be a revolutionary socialist, was really a true fascist and a rabid anti-Semitic racist.

In his Paris newspaper, *L'Oeuvre,* he staged violent attacks on the ministers at Vichy, calling them "an anonymous clique," "intriguers without credentials" and so on. Pétain, who was angered by those excesses agreed in principle to have Déat arrested. Du Moulin phoned General La Laurencie on that same day, December 9, to carry out the arrest as soon as he received the special password: "The Marshal's wife has reached the demarcation line."

Pétain actually viewed politics more as a struggle between individuals than one of ideas. As a replacement for Laval the best man was thought to be former prime minister Pierre-Etienne Flandin who arrived at Vichy on December 6. These events made up the poisonous atmosphere of the temporary capital. "There are only attacks and counter attacks, secret meetings, plots, intrigues and conspiracies." as Alfred Mallet, Laval's secretary and biographer, would note.

At the same time, Pétain, in his small office next to his bedroom that sported a lamp in the shape of the "Francisque," suddenly decided to write a letter to Hitler to inform the Führer of his dismissal of Laval. General La Laurencie was to hand the letter to Otto Abetz on the following day, but during the night the Marshal had a change of heart and he decided that it was a bad idea to give Laval's accomplice Abetz any kind of advance notice.

The operation was probably scheduled to take place within a few days, around December 12. But then suddenly came the "coup de théâtre" with the announcement that the Aiglon's remains were about to be returned by Germany and that event set off a palace revolt.

4.

Political Struggle at Vichy

"Laval set himself up as the rightful heir, but old men don't like heirs."
Henri Moysset

The Vichy government was not the first to be informed of this surprising news. At four in the afternoon on December 10, General La Laurencie was summoned by Pierre Laval to the Hôtel Matignon in Paris. His account deserves to be reproduced in its entirety:

> I was immediately ushered into the minister's office where Ambassador de Brinon was waiting. Mr. Laval visibly ecstatic was holding a letter from the Führer informing Marshal Pétain that he was returning the remains of the Duke of Reichstadt to France.
>
> The deputy prime minister [Laval] told me about the German chancellor's decision but he insisted in such an

undignified manner about the nobility of the gesture and went on in exaggerated terms about the form of the Führer's letter—which was indeed beautifully presented—that I felt extremely ill at ease. We then discussed the details of the ceremony of the return of the remains and Mr. Pierre Laval told me:

The casket will arrive at the railroad station on Saturday, December 14 at midnight. German troops will escort it through Paris and deliver it to the French authorities at the Invalides. The Führer wants the ceremony to be particularly magnificent and, as you may appreciate his thoughtfulness, the Marshal will be present at the ceremony and shall personally receive the remains of the Emperor's son. The chancellor is adamant about this. Furthermore an infantry battalion will present arms to the Marshal as he arrives by train and the Marshal will also inspect a second battalion on the Place Vauban.

And Mr. Pierre Laval underscored his words with unbearably vulgar gestures[88] as he enjoyed repeating the details of the ceremony. He could not understand that to have honors paid to the head of the French state by German units in the French capital was something rather shocking."

The rather naïve General de la Laurencie was not very subtle but he understood the meaning of dignity.

I found it impossible to hide my indignation and said to Mr. Laval: "Mr. President, how can you do such a thing to the Marshal! Are you trying to destroy his image with public opinion? Can't you see how painful it could be to the French people that on the occasion of his first trip to Paris the Marshal will review German army units? My heart as a soldier is revolted by such a thought." Seeking to help his

---

88. The general and the politician obviously came from different social circles.

master, de Brinon had the gall to say: "I don't understand the reason for your indignation general. At Montoire the Marshal did revue a company that was presenting arms!"

I answered the Ambassador very coldly: "Mr. Ambassador you do not understand! I am very surprised that you wouldn't see the difference between the meeting at Montoire and the Marshal traveling to Paris. In any case the Marshal will not come."

Mr. Laval then became flustered: "If the Marshal fails to appear it will be a personal insult to the Führer with very serious consequences."

Laval did have a law degree but he was far from well read and had no interest in history other than that of his own region. He felt no attraction to the memory of Napoleon and his son. Had he even ever visited the Invalides? The idea of that spectacular return didn't originate with him as Tournoux had mistakenly surmised. The initial Benoist-Méchin inspiration and Arno Breker's recollections are more plausible. Actually, as Abetz would confirm, it was Hitler himself—whom Pétain had labeled "a dangerous mediocrity"—who had decided on the return of the ashes. But why, what could his motivation be? It has been said that it was to appease the French people and to encourage them to embrace collaboration with a generous and victorious Germany. But as the four years of occupation were to demonstrate, the German dictator sought to subjugate and exploit France in ways that would only increase until the gradual collapse of Nazi Germany. It is therefore more realistic to see the return of the ashes of the Aiglon as a spur of the moment decision intended on Hitler's part to glorify and identify him with Napoleon. However, he was to garnish more scorn than glory for himself.

As for the tricky Laval, he had understood the situation immediately and was determined to use it to his own advantage.

Hitler's historical and useless dream could be a major step in the direction that Laval would seek to go so stubbornly right up to the end. He wanted to present this goal to Marshal Pétain and to the French people as a spectacular and solemn understanding towards a Franco-German alliance—something Laval would still strive for three years later. The return of the Aiglon would help erase the disastrous effects that Montoire had on French public opinion and the utter failure of that policy.

Then de Brinon with his predatory face had another idea: have Hitler come to Paris on December 15 as well and parade with Pétain up the Champs Elysées since the Führer wanted "to be a new Charlemagne and do better than Napoleon." What more would France have to endure following the terrible events of June 1940?

The two partners in crime, Laval and de Brinon, thought that the French people would be won over by such a chivalrous gesture and would enthusiastically accept the collaboration policy.

"Well what do you think?" asked Laval as he tossed as usual his half-smoked cigarette butt. "That's even better than the granting of a few kilos of potatoes or even freeing prisoners of war who have four children!"

Yet, Laval had to act cautiously and cleverly as he knew best and wanted Brinon to find out what the mood at Vichy was like. On the next day December 11, Brinon phoned the Hotel du Parc at Vichy to announce that after many rejections the German government finally accepted that the head of the French state be installed at Versailles.[89] This would apply only to Marshal Pétain alone and not his government, which immediately created a kind of panic. Was this a maneuver to take advantage and isolate the old Marshal into the role of a figurehead and impose a new cabinet filled with unconditional

---

89. The prefect of the department of Seine-et-Oise had prepared a stately mansion at 9 avenue de la Reine in the city of Versailles, with a room painted blue for the Marshal and one in pink for his wife.

collaborators? Pétain's reaction was: "This is another one of Laval's ideas!"

His unacceptable position changed a few minutes later after a second phone call from Brinon that Germany was returning the remain of the Aiglon to France.[90]

King Louis-Philippe had decided upon and requested the return of the remains of the great emperor in 1840. One hundred years later his successor Marshal Pétain, without any prior consultations or request on his part, was simply informed of the return of the body of Napoleon's son. The difference was symbolic of the subjugation to which France was reduced as a vassal state within Hitler's Europe.

No one at Vichy had given any thought to the Duke of Reichstadt and most people didn't even know where he was actually buried. They surely must have scurried around looking for an encyclopedia to refresh their memory. The sudden appearance of that ghost among the uncertain policies of the Vichy government would completely change the rules of the game and serve as the main excuse for the dismissal of Pierre Laval. While the overthrow of Laval had been discussed, those in favor were hesitant about taking action. The long shadow of the Emperor's son suddenly set off a palace revolt with national implications originating at Vichy's Hotel du Parc with its decorated salons and their blue and pink wallpaper motifs of rosy cherubs. One hundred years after his death, Napoleon II was suddenly making an appearance.

---

90. The German initiative that Hitler thought up and decided came across a French attempt that would then fail. At the start of 1939 the association *la Sabretache* created a committee to commemorate the return of Napoleon's ashes that included generals Weygand, Bricard, Koechlin-Schwartz and Edouard Driault. A monument adorned with an eagle taken from the Tuileries gates and its inauguration on the banks of the Seine on December 15 with General La Laurencie and Pierre Laval. Invitations were printed up but on December 12 the German authorities refused permission for the ceremony. See André Desfeuilles, *Autour d'un centenaire manqué.*

The small temporary capital of France was to find out later on that the entire ceremony had been thought up and prepared in Germany without discussing any of the details with its original promoter, Jacques Benoist-Méchin: the opening of the crypt, the terms of the transfer and the arrival in Paris. A prisoner of the Germans since the armistice, Benoist-Méchin had published a successful anti-war book, *La Moisson de Quarante*. He was freed on August 15, 1940, and, as a great admirer of Marshal Pétain, he was appointed head of the prisoners of war commission in Berlin in the fall. Actually he was serving as the deputy to Scapini and doing very useful work in Germany. Since the Habsbourg family heirs had lost title to the crypt, the German authorities had prepared the transfer operation on their own initiative without informing Benoist-Méchin. Fearing negative reactions on the part of the Parisians, the Wilhelmstrasse didn't want the operation taking place in broad daylight.[91] It was to take place at night in a Paris that was under curfew and in any case, nighttime processions and ceremonies by torchlight were part and parcel of the Nazi ritual.

The phone conversations with de Brinon continued in Marshal Pétain's office. The ambassador of defeat was asking that the head of state be present at the Invalides to welcome the remains of the prince who was to join his father. In the past President Poincaré had written of Pétain in his memoirs as "the most defeatist of our military leaders." Had Pétain agreed to be present in—the Invalides—architect Hardouin-Mansart's masterpiece that would have symbolized the triumph of Franco-German understanding even more than the meeting at the small country railroad station of Montoire. France would have then descended to the status of a vassal state of Nazi Germany and endured a humiliation greater than any that Napoleon had

---

91 The "Wilhelmstrasse" was the familiar name of the German Foreign Ministry after the avenue where it was located in the government district in Berlin.

inflicted on the vanquished kings of Europe. The Emperor's son was going to provide the pretext for such a celebration!

However Pétain didn't welcome the invitation one bit. To inform him four days before! To subject a man of his age and stature to such treatment, to have him formally inspect two German battalions during his first visit to "his" own capital city, one at the railroad station upon arrival, and the second on the Place Vauban was nothing short of outrageous. None of this was acceptable and Pétain understood that Hitler intended to compromise him. He answered de Brinon, whom he found somewhat despicable, in the same manner Louis XIV referred to his predecessor: "I shall see."

As de Brinon kept on insisting, Pétain, who by then was ready to go to lunch was becoming very impatient, cut short the conversation by pretending to agree.

At the same time General Doyen phoned his good friend General Laure:

"I hear you are traveling with your boss on Sunday. Correct?"

"Yes."

"Well, make sure the trip does not take place. I can't say any more. Please do what you can to prevent this trip."

That same day—December 11—Abetz called Benoist-Méchin who was about to leave for Berlin:

"Your greatest wish is about to come true."

And he found out that the transfer was approved and would take place on December 15.

"In four days?"

"Correct. It must remain top secret but all the details have been worked out."

"This can't happen!" replied Benoist-Méchin, all flustered. "Don't do it! The time isn't appropriate! What was good in 1938 is no longer so today!"

Later, Benoist-Méchin would write: "how could we be happy with the return of a ghost while so many others were still prisoners of war?"

There followed a long conversation and Abetz confirmed that the decision was irrevocable and that Pétain would also be there. "You are an incurable romantic!" said the now-frustrated originator of the idea. "I can assure you that it will have a completely opposite effect and that we shall be up against even more problems!"

"It's too late," said Abetz whose enthusiasm was beginning to wane. "The train has already left Vienna and will soon arrive at Compiègne." Discouraged and very displeased Benoist-Méchin returned to Berlin where he later learned that Laval had been dismissed, that Pétain did not come to the ceremony, and that only Abetz was present...[92]

In Paris however the enthusiasm displayed by the collaborators was at its height. To drum up interest for the forgotten son of Napoleon, Brinon asked Maurice Rostand to write a poem as a kind of epilog to his father's famous play.[93]

---

92. Benoist-Méchin joined the Vichy government as under secretary of state for foreign affairs in February 1941, two months after the return of the Aiglon and would be fired by Laval in 1942 because of his ultra-collaborationism, an exceptional case. The two men didn't like each other. He was arrested at the Liberation of France and was condemned to death by the High Court in 1947 and then pardoned by President Auriol and freed in 1954 after a period of imprisonment at Saint-Martin de Ré. He became a historian of the Arabs and wrote several books, *Mustapha Kemal, Ibn Saud*. The French government used his services in various Arab countries after 1958. He died in 1983. The author had lunch with him and Sir Oswald Mosley, the infamous former head of the British fascists, and Lady Mosley (née Mitford) at the magnificent Mosley estate in England. Birds of a feather...

93. Edmond Rostand's play *L'Aiglon* is in six acts, an exceptional length for a theatrical work. The famous economist Alfred Sauvy at the time of the return of the remains wrote a mocking satirical seventh act. A few verses where Hitler addresses the Aiglon in his casket:

> You who were for the Empire a cause for regret
> Who had Metternich and Austria trembling,
> Tortured ghost with a too rich past

The effeminate old man faded and wearing heavy make up who was seen taking the last metro accompanying his very old mother, agreed and took the task to heart: fifteen stanzas with six verses each. It starts as follows:

> Now…Now that the war is over
> Now that the hope of future harmony
> Can take the place of our regrets,
> Now that the star with the Goddess' name
> Will never again shine in a stormy sky
> On our dead youth,
>
> Full of sad reality and legend
> In the white uniform of his rank,
> There is a blond prisoner
> Whose return we have dreamed of for years,
> A prince whose strange fate
> It was to have death as his cure
>
> More than one century of exile for such a short life
> It was long for a heart suffering in the distance
> Far from our perilous destinies!
> Can he not return to his clear landscape
> And can we not let the door of the cage
> Be opened for Napoleon two?[94]

Obviously this wasn't even close to Victor Hugo:
"Sire, you shall return to your capital…"
In poetry as in glory there had been a decline in quality.

> Who became entranced at the word Wagram,
> Your dream is about to come true,
> Son of Napoleon: go avenge your father
> Come help us in France to defeat England!
>   Alfred Sauvy *Humour et politique* Paris 1979

94. The ode was published in its entirety in *Paris-Soir* on Monday, December 16, 1940. (Author's collection.)

The following day, December 12, Marshal Pétain said:

"The news doesn't surprise me that much. La Laurencie sent me the same information by secret emissary. He assures me it is the great inside news of the day and that I shouldn't move at all."

"The Germans have strange ideas," said General Laure, none too subtle but earnest.

"They can have all the ideas they wish, but if they think I will show up as a prisoner in Paris next to Hitler they don't know me well enough! I don't want the Paris newspapers to publish my pictures in the midst of German soldiers…"

After all the Duke of Reichstadt had never commanded more than a regiment while he, Pétain, had been commander in chief of the entire French army just like Napoleon…

That evening Laure wrote in his diary:

"This morning Laval and Brinon were insisting. We made it very clear [meaning Laure and du Moulin] that the Marshal could return to the capital only in response to a call by the people and not on the invitation by the Führer, whatever the reason may be. Also his age and rank do not allow him to improvise such a trip that would interrupt his duties for several days. Laval and Brinon are obviously very uncomfortable because of our resistance. They go so far as to say that Hitler will send a message asking the Marshal to attend the ceremony. We answer that they must do all they can to prevent the invitation from being sent since the head of state could not reply in the affirmative."[95]

At around 5 p.m. Laval called from Paris to speak with du Moulin who transcribed their conversation:

"So it's you?" said Laval

"Yes, Mr. President."

---

95. Quoted by Henri Amouroux.

"Well the idea of the Marshal's trip to Paris is making progress. The Germans no longer oppose his transfer to Versailles."

"They are being very good about it."

"What are you saying?"

"I'm saying they are being very good."

"I don't understand…oh yes…But I think we should move things along somewhat faster. I am returning to Vichy tomorrow. I would really like to take the Marshal back with me. What do you think?"

"I don't think the Marshal needs you to return to Paris."

"What?"

"He will return on his own."

"Say, what's the matter with you?"

"I am rather eager to speak to you man to man, Mr. President. Things are getting out of hand. The atmosphere is very heavy and I tend to think you have something to do with it."

"Me?"

"Yes, your little friends are beginning to bother us quite a bit."

Laval hangs up the phone.

Even though du Moulin was often prone to attributing a major role to himself after the fact, the dialog as cited is basically correct. The Marshal's chief of staff had not hesitated in taking that kind of attitude because he had been the first to understand that the Aiglon's return, as Peyrouton said "was the opportunity they had been looking for several weeks to take action against Laval." When he understood that the people at Vichy were beginning to turn against him, Laval immediately warned Abetz about Pétain. The German ambassador replied: "If the Marshal doesn't come to an invitation by the chancellor it will be taken as a personal insult."

Laval had only one solution confident as he was in his ability as a negotiator. Accompanied by de Brinon in his new uniform as an ambassador (military cap with oak leaves and gold braided tunic) he boarded the train from Paris to Vichy at 11 p.m. where they arrived the next morning, December 13.

Perhaps the spectacular operation of the return of the remains of the Aiglon actually contains two intentions that are not mutually exclusive:

For Hitler this was simply a new milestone in the pursuit of his dream. To be the one to return the Duke of Reichstadt to his father, the Emperor, in his glorious temple, in the presence of a defeated Marshal of France among the shadows of other Napoleonic marshals who had defeated his country—Germany—was clearly a form of revenge and another victory. At the same time it was a way to compensate Pétain for Hitler's refusal to take him to Versailles with his ministers, contrary to the armistice agreement, and the symbolic sealing of the Franco-German alliance against England, the hereditary enemy. But he didn't realize that the French people knew the Duke of Windsor much better than they remembered the Duke of Reichstadt.

To Laval and his accomplices there was the prospect of moving Pétain to Versailles in a purely decorative role, almost sequestered like the Aiglon at the palace at Schoenbrunn. At Matignon under Laval's leadership as prime minister a new purged and modified government (where Brinon perhaps saw himself as minister of foreign affairs?) would emerge. This was something Laval had wanted for a long time, so that he could continue to collaborate with impunity in every sense of the word.

Both programs were based on the same assumption: that Marshal Pétain would come to Paris and then move into Versailles as a virtual hostage "relieved of power in favor of the successor he had imprudently named" as Delpierre de Bayac wrote. But on that morning of December 13, Pétain, "whose willpower needed to be wound up like an alarm clock" as Henri Amouroux wrote, hadn't yet taken a firm position. That day would turn out to be decisive from one hour to the next. At ten in the morning the head of state met with Bouthillier and informed him of two decisions: he was not going to Paris and he would not dismiss Laval. The shadow of the Aiglon would not guide France and Germany into a criminal partnership. Regarding the issue of collaboration the conspirators therefore had to start from scratch.

Pétain was actually not very much concerned with Napoleon's son. A cultured man who spoke several languages, he appeared to be more interested in literature than in history. Like all the graduates of the École de Guerre he knew the plans of the battle of Austerlitz by heart but was far from having Hitler's admiration for Napoleon. Politically, Pétain was an old republican even though he was well aware of being the successor of every French ruler and king to whom he felt he was the equal. He even imitated the formal words used by the sovereigns "We, Marshal of France, head of the French state." He had no interest in any other pretenders to the throne. Pétain paid no attention to the Orléans family—and would treat the count of Paris when he came to visit or the descendants of Napoleon who at the time were represented by a young man of whom Pétain had never heard of with little regard. How could he ever imagine that as the first head of the French state to be imprisoned since Napoleon, he eventually would end up like him on a small island and a town named after the Prince of Joinville who had engineered the return of the remains of Napoleon?

Laval and Brinon arrived at the hotel du Parc at twelve thirty and ran into the Marshal who was in a good mood as he was beginning his morning walk. The deputy prime minister, informal as he usually was, told Pétain he was going to have lunch at his home at Châteldon and that Brinon would remain to explain matters. Laval made an appointment to see the Marshal later in the afternoon. At one Brinon gave the Marshal Hitler's letter containing a personal invitation:

Berlin, 13 December 1940

Marshal,

December 15 will be the one hundredth anniversary of the day when the body of Napoleon was brought to the Invalides. I wish to take this opportunity to inform you, Marshal, that I have made the decision to return to the French people the remains of the Duke of Reichstadt. Thus, the son of Napoleon will leave a place which during his tragic life was foreign to him to return to his homeland to rest near his illustrious father. Marshal, I address you the expression of my personal esteem.

Signed: Adolf Hitler

Brinon attempted to entice the old man by describing the trip and how comfortable it would be while also addressing the dangers of any refusal that could spark a very dangerous situation. Pétain, who was by now in a hurry to go to lunch, cut him short, he was a hearty eater but had the habit of diluting his wine with water.

5.

Napoleon II Victorious

The victor of Verdun—an expression the old Marshal always enjoyed hearing—often experienced absences and forgetfulness during the day and his doctor, Dr. Ménétrel, recommended that he take a nap after lunch. It was during that time that the crisis took a sharp turn.

Early in the afternoon after lunch, Bouthillier and Peyrouton met in the passageway between the hotels du Parc and the Majestic and went for a stroll on the banks of the Allier River to exchange the latest news that confirmed the need for very quick action. Bouthillier had learned the details of the military conference of November 29 from Admiral Darlan. There was no time to waste since the ministers felt their positions were threatened and there was the rumor of a government that would include Laval, Luchaire, Déat, and Doriot.

Peyrouton (or as du Moulin described him, "the happy tough guy") also told Bouthillier about the latest happenings and in particular, the Marshal's apparent change of mind:

"Everything is up in the air. The Marshal is going to Paris. Brinon and Laval have won. There is also talk of going to Rouen. The Marshal will leave alone with Laval."

After some thought Bouthillier said:

"It has to be done tonight."

The return of the Aiglon was to crystallize the dismissal of Laval. It was during that conversation that the idea of arresting Laval was discussed for the first time.

"I'll have him arrested so he can't call on Abetz and his crew for help," said Peyrouton.

So they decided to take action without waiting any longer. As Henri Amouroux described it

"On that day in the few hours when fateful decisions were made, the anti-Laval conspirators were to be the most decisive, quick and enterprising. The conspiracy had been set up for several days during discussions that were kept essentially secret and could therefore make the action successful. The goal was the same as Laval's, namely to control Marshal Pétain. The group that would speak last was assured of succeeding. "Seizing an old man" as they all repeated several times over a description that fit the circumstances perfectly."

Feeling rested after his nap, Pétain received Laval who had returned from Châteldon and de Brinon in the ballroom with the three windows where he usually received his visitors and called in du Moulin. The deputy prime minister whose white shirt and tie enhanced his swarthy complexion sounded off triumphantly:

"The Führer, Marshal, has decided to offer France a big surprise, a great surprise, and a magnificent gift. On the one hundredth anniversary of the return [of Napoleon] from Saint-Helena, the ashes of the Duke of Reichstadt that were resting in the Capuchins church in Vienna. You know that he is Austrian by birth."

"Not at all!" said Pétain thinking about the Aiglon.

"But yes, Hitler is Austrian and he is even a catholic. He never liked pre-Anschluss Vienna, you know, the Vienna of the archdukes, the ballerinas, the Jews (but that was the Aiglon's Vienna as well…). He is also obsessed with the legend of the Emperor. He is convinced that nothing will captivate the French people more than the return of the ashes of the Aiglon.

"Something to consider," said Pétain, without taking a position and, as was his habit, moving pencils and pens around to line them up perfectly.

"But Marshal, you have to be present. If you are not there the dramatic effect will be lost."

"But I have no business being present! Can you picture me in Paris during this cold season in the midst of Germans as I preside over a ceremony the French people will not even comprehend."

The victor of Verdun refused to show up in front of a forest of flags with swastikas. Montoire had been a lesson of what that kind of humiliation could be.

According to Albert Mallet, Laval was careful to answer:

"First: create the atmosphere. He detailed two separate ceremonies: on Saturday night the casket would be handed over at the gates of the Invalides under torchlight and then on Sunday morning there would be a ceremony inside the church."

Pétain would be present only at the second event and the deputy prime minister drew a picture of the Marshal in front of the tomb of Napoleon, his predecessor. The old soldier by then was seduced by the thought of being present in all his glory, something he loved very dearly.

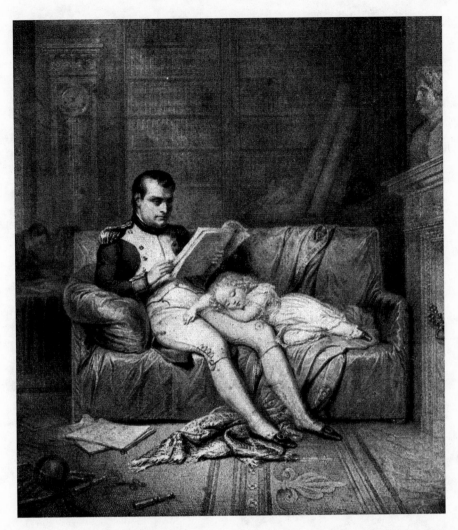

The Eagle and his Eaglet, father and son.

Napoleon II was officially Emperor of the French for two weeks in 1815.

In the crypt of the Austrian emperors in Vienna the sarcophagus of the Duke of Reichstadt is ready to be taken to Paris.

Hitler ordered the railroad car be turned into a memorial chapel.

above
In Paris German soldiers under torchlights place the heavy sarcophagus on an artillery caisson..

below
Two German soldiers guarding the railroad car bearing the coat of arms of the Duke of Reichstadt.

above
The caisson is hitched to a tractor.

below
German ambassador Otto Abetz officially handing over the casket of Napoleon II to the representatives of Marshal Pétain, Admiral Jean François Darlan, and General Laure.

above

The ceremony held on December 15 was attended by a few officials and a select group of guests.

right

The dramatic draping of the sarcophagus in the French flag and flowers around Napoleon's tomb.

left

The last government of the Third Republic. *From the left:* General Weygand, Foreign Minister Paul Baudoin, Paul Reynaud, and Marshal Pétain. May 1940.

above
Marshal Philippe Pétain, official portrait
as Head of State in 1940.

right
Hitler in Paris during his early morning
visit on June 17, 1940, with Albert Speer
(left) and sculptor Arno Brecker.

above
Hitler and Göring at Compiègne for the
signing of the armistice on June 23, 1940,
in the railroad car.

left
Hitler at Napoleon's tomb.

below
Hitler admires the cathedral of
Strasbourg, June 1940.

above

The French sign the armistice inside the railroad car at Compiègne. Hitler is at the left, Rudolf Hess is center, facing the camera, and the French delegation is on the right. June 23, 1940.

below

The meeting at Montoire on October 24, 1940.

Marcel Déat *(center)* with fellow collaborators Alphonse de Chateaubriant *(left)* and Paul Chack *(right)*.

above
Ambassador Otto Abetz.

right
Jacques Benoist-Méchin.

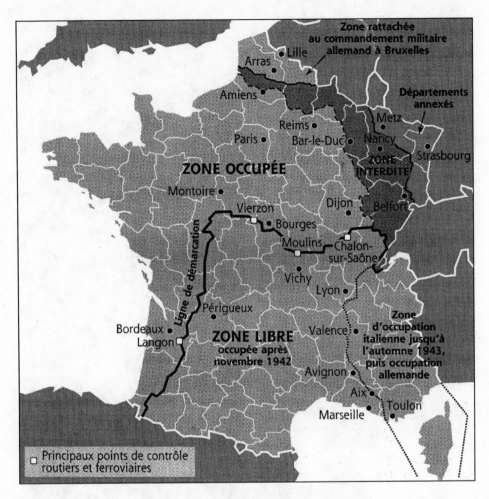

Zone rattachée
au commandement militaire
allemand à Bruxelles

Départements
annexés

Arras
Lille
Amiens
Reims
Paris
Bar-le-Duc
Metz
Nancy
Strasbourg
ZONE OCCUPÉE
ZONE
INTERDITE
Montoire
Dijon
Belfort
Vierzon
Bourges
Moulins
Chalon-
sur-Saône
Ligne de démarcation
Vichy
Lyon
Périgueux
Bordeaux
Langon
ZONE LIBRE
occupée après
novembre 1942
Valence
Zone
d'occupation
italienne jusqu'à
l'automne 1943,
puis occupation
allemande
Avignon
Aix
Toulon
Marseille

☐ Principaux points de contrôle
routiers et ferroviaires

above
France divided into three zones, with Vichy
in charge of the southern "free zone" until
November 1942.

left
German checkpoint at the demarcation line.

Pierre Laval in 1940.

above
Minister of the Interior
Marcel Peyrouton.

right
Xavier Vallat, the first Commissioner
for Jewish affairs, at Vichy.

General Charles De Gaulle in London, 1940.

above
Hitler in a command car on the Champs Elysées,
June 23, 1940.

left
Hitler and his entourage leave the
chapel of the Invalides where he
visited Napoleon's tomb.

above
L'*Aiglon* was a fashionable restaurant in the rue de Berri in Paris during the occupation.

below
Pétain, Hitler, and Ribbentrop at Montoire railroad station meet in the Führer's railway car on October 24, 1940.

Fernand de Brinon, Vichy's ambassador to the German occupation
authorities, meets with General von Stülpnagel in 1940.

With his back to the mahogany library with its doors covered in green silk, the Head of State looked like "a fortress under siege," always ready to agree with the person who was lecturing him; he was slowly wavering from refusing to travel to considering the possibility. "I can picture you there quite clearly, Marshal," said Laval, "and then this is something you can't refuse. It would be the equivalent of a personal insult to Hitler."

"So that's it, I'm always forced to do something, like at Montoire?"

"Don't get angry, Marshal. I am speaking in your best interest. In any case if this doesn't suit you, I will not fight over a ceremony. I will fight for the big things. But it would be a shame! Everything is ready. The body will arrive at the Gare de l'Est late Saturday night then it will be taken on an artillery caisson to the expanse of the Invalides, into the Emperor's tomb at night under the torches. The Germans like that sort of thing. It reminds them of Wagner and romantic nights. I'm sure you don't find it shocking. I think it's very beautiful."

"Especially if Hitler is not present."

"He will not be there! He knows that his presence would be misunderstood and he doesn't want to hurt anyone's feelings. In any case the Germans will not enter the crypt. They will stop on the steps of the church. You shall be alone below, with the French."

Laval had never been so persuasive with the Marshal who was surprised by the eloquence and gave in.

"Well, so be it! Get things ready. When do we go?"

"Tomorrow morning by special train, three or four carriages."

"Which ministers will be coming with me?"

"There will be no ministers; they are not well liked in Paris and the Germans don't trust them."

Isolated, Pétain could then be forced into making changes in his cabinet. He became reticent once again.

"But I shall be alone."

"Alone? Not at all, I'll be there, Marshal," said Laval. "And your entourage will be with you. Take General Laure, du Moulin, Ménétrel and above all, military men, as many as you like because it is a ceremony."

"And what will I do afterwards?"

Once the principle was agreed to they went into the details. Pétain refused to sleep at the Elysée Palace which he hated and preferred the Trianon at Versailles where he remembered spending time with a few girlfriends. But he finally agreed to Matignon because it had central heating.

"I'll give you my room," replied Laval magnanimously.

Then there was the issue of meals. The Marshal usually patronized the Café de Paris and wished to have lunch there following the Sunday morning ceremony.

At that point Brinon pointed out that there was a protocol problem. The Marshal gave in and agreed to have lunch at Matignon but only on condition that his favorite chef would compose the menu and that he be able to invite his personal friends whom he longed to see after six long months spent at Vichy. Brinon proposed Jean Thierry, Pétain's former orderly, and Achille Murat who would be invited as the representative of the great dignitaries of the Empire. Pétain agreed; then Brinon insisted for an immediate answer to the Führer's letter. At that point du Moulin injected himself into the conversation to gain some time. But Brinon was convinced that he had succeeded and telephoned his secretary who was also his mistress at Matignon to send out invitations for lunch on December 15.

After that exchange with Brinon, Laval kept on talking to the Marshal:

"You shall go out for a walk in Paris the following day, on the boulevard des Invalides no less, in civilian clothes, with your walking stick. Everyone will recognize you and pay their respects." Laval knew how to entice Pétain. "You'll go back to your apartment on Latour-Maubourg square and even take a tour of the occupied zone."

Du Moulin de Labarthète who was to be part of the Marshal's entourage commented with sarcasm:

"The Marshal is very much interested in the trip. Laval feels Pétain has been won over, Brinon's nose seemed to hook even more with pleasure. The Marshal asks for a map. He unfolds it on the table and begins to plan a possible itinerary. "Yes a triangular trip: Rouen, Alençon, Bourges, maybe Nevers. My train could stop in Le Mans for the night. What do you think?" For a few minutes the conversations get lost in such details. Newsmen from the southern zone will be driven to Paris in two buses using a collective "ausweis." Laval would later write, "I left the Marshal on the friendliest of terms."

So it appeared that the matter was agreed upon. France's subordination, of which Pétain was the symbol, would then be proclaimed at the feet of the victor of Jena and the ghost of the poor Aiglon would make it happen as the final calamity of a life filled with sorrow.

However Laval had not planned on the return of the conspirators and had forgotten Adrien Marquet's words the day he had fired him: "You engineered everything, you bastard! You just opened the door through which you shall also pass!"

Following their conversation, Bouthillier and Peyrouton had quickly rounded up all their co-conspirators. They all met at du Moulin's apartment that—like all the other guests at the hotel, even the best known among them—also served as his office, with wooden flats over the bathtub used as a table and current files stored in the bidet, more files were piled up under the bed and the night table was turned into a safe. In that tiny space Darlan and Baudoin followed by Alibert who also squeezed in with other ministers: General Huntziger, the "anachronistic"

Caziot as Marcel Déat would describe him, and Admiral Platon whose political destiny would end in tragedy.[96]

The rebels took stock of the situation. Besides the highly symbolic character of the ceremony that was obviously meant to enshrine Franco-German understanding they could sense that it was an opportunity for Laval to isolate Pétain at Versailles afterward and keep him hostage, far from his ministers, forcing upon him a new government of extremists. Then with their help Laval would go as fast as possible down the path of collaboration using the patronage of the old soldier. Even though the Swiss diplomat Walter Stucki thought so, it was unlikely that Laval at this time wished to be surrounded by the "ultra-collaborationists" whom he would be forced to accept later on: Marcel Déat, Philippe Henriot, and Joseph Darnand.

Laval would have been satisfied to be able to eliminate even a few of his enemies. But the conspirators feared the worse from any governmental change of venue. They concluded that they must deprive the return of the Aiglon of its symbolic effect at all costs, prevent Pétain from taking the trip and eliminate Laval as if Napoleon II were returning to claim his throne and had immediately decided to send the modern-day Fouché into exile. As du Moulin would say, the conspiracy of the ministers was merely a counter-plot and Henri Amouroux wrote:

"Unable to accept Laval's increasingly cavalier attitude and his relationship with Abetz, the ministers thought that by getting rid of the man who was the symbol of collaboration they would acquire greater independence from the German occupiers, improve their image with the Americans and the British and regain the confidence of French public opinion."

Meeting in a small room in the Hotel du Parc General Huntziger at first showed some reticence and spoke of the consequences if the Germans got angry, as he anticipated, that made

---

96. He was executed by the FFI (Forces Françaises de l'Intérieur) in 1944, some said by being dismembered and torn apart by two automobiles.

a strong impression. Bouthillier however made his point quite forcefully with the support of Alibert who was sitting in front of the mirror of the armoire as he continuously smoked his cigars.

"Get on with it, gentlemen, tomorrow it will be too late…"

He was also helped by Peyrouton who not only wanted Laval fired but placed under arrest by his policemen, he knew he could get it done and was ready to assume full responsibility. The Marshal would then acquire tremendous stature from the daring action and the minister was requesting a unanimous vote.

In the tense atmosphere one hand after the other went up including that of Darlan who, true to his reputation as the "silent Gascon," had been quietly smoking his pipe in the background. After a short moment of hesitation Huntziger also agreed. That kind of unanimity produced a dramatic change in the course of events and avoided tainting the return of the Emperor's son with shame. That vote actually paved the way for Napoleon II's victory.

The conspirators felt they were acting to save the country and included those who hoped that once Laval was out of the way Flandin (whom Laval referred to as "that long nothing-ness") would also bow out. Bouthillier, the main mover in the conspiracy, could not do more and seems to have had no other goal than a day to day management of the administration that remained strictly within the confines of the armistice. Peyrouton the quintessential political adventurer who had been involved with many different groups was possibly thinking that he could succeed where Laval had failed by being more combative, more of a team player and more concerned with eliciting Marshal Pétain's confidence. Baudoin would have been satisfied to return to his former post as foreign minister after having been dismissed; Huntziger only sought a military role, and worried about having to take part in an unjust and uncertain war. But by far the most ambitious among the plotters was Jean François Darlan who had built and led a powerful fleet that remained intact and who therefore felt able, since there was no indication he could avenge Trafalgar, to lead the government and the state. However he wasn't convinced that his time had come, it would indeed do so later on and seal his doom.

On December 13 a group of top government functionaries who were used to obeying orders would suddenly have to behave like politicians and even revolutionaries. Later on Dr. Martin who headed the secret services and Dr. Bernard Ménétrel, who was Pétain's personal physician, also arrived. The former was proposing to act very expeditiously against Laval either by a court martial that would have its sentence executed that same night (the same procedure would be used two years later with the murderer of Admiral Darlan) or a summary execution much like Corneliu Codreanu the Romanian Iron Guard fascist leader shot by King Carol's police in 1938. But Martin did not want to be mixed up in the execution: these after all, were not the days of the Duke of Enghien who was executed on Napoleon's orders. Dr. Ménétrel, according to du Moulin, had a different plan in mind: to have Laval shot unexpectedly during his arrest as it often happens in conspiracies. If that scenario had prevailed France's fate would have been sealed: Marshal Pétain would have been deported to Germany, the entire country occupied and ruled by a Gauleiter. The question remains as to whether such an outcome would that have been better or worse for the country in the long run?

The discussion was becoming ridiculous and it was high time for caution to prevail. Peyrouton knew the Marshal: he would never want to have Laval's blood on his hands there would be other occasions when he would be compelled to accept it. Arresting Laval was bold enough and Darlan was very clear that it be done with every possible courtesy. The Admiral was also asked to speak to Pétain as the representative of the conspirators.

At 4:45 p.m. they went to see the Marshal. "He understood; his blue eyes were cold and unblinking. He didn't say a word as the ministers sat around the flimsy round table" wrote Albert Mallet. With his choppy way of speaking Darlan who was hiding his pipe in the presence of Pétain, proceeded in a few clipped sentences to condemn Laval's policies and "concluded by saying that the head of state could not appear in Paris next to Laval" as Bouthillier reported. Then Darlan recalled:

"The Marshal stroked his mustache, thought for a moment, and then told us:

"I have made my decision. He must resign."

So it was decided: Marshal Pétain refused to play the role of Grand Marshal Bertrand who was replaced by a nonentity like Grouchy.[97]

Peyrouton produced a set of files containing documents that were damning for Laval while Bouthillier discussed the Paris newspapers and in particular the latest front page of Marcel Déat's newspaper *L'Oeuvre* where he wrote: "You can recognize the German generals by their lapels. The French generals also, but they are not the same ones."[98]

A particularly painful truth, no doubt, but Pétain didn't admit any criticism of the army and was therefore incensed: "Laval is the one encouraging all this. Well, this is it, we have to stop it!"

And as Bouthillier noted in his memoirs:

"He knew that he could no longer hesitate but he also couldn't forget that the Germans were at Moulins."

No doubt Pétain reached a decision at that precise moment. The choice of military ceremony at the Invalides and a walk in

---

97 General Grouchy is usually blamed for Napoleon's defeat at Waterloo when his cavalry regiment failed to arrive in time to counterattack. His name was popularized by Victor Hugo in his poem entitled "Waterloo."
98. Play on words in French: "revers" (lapels or cuffs) can also mean losses. In other words, French generals are known mainly for losing battles.

the streets of Paris alone since it was out of the question for him to bring his wife and running the risk of being locked up in the palace of Versailles, like some do nothing figurehead owing obedience to an all powerful Laval, he could no longer hesitate. He must rid himself at the same time of the evil genius and do without the triumph of the Aiglon who suddenly became the true victor of this battle. What Déat would describe as "a comic scene out of a side show or a burlesque" actually turned out to be one of the key episodes of the history of those years.

Du Moulin would comment about Pétain: "I was surprised by his firm resolve. The same man who appeared to be weakening just one hour before—unless he was acting to the hilt—now appeared to have the resolve of a lion." He was swayed by his ministers and gave in finally to the pent up disgust that he felt for Laval.

"Mr. Laval is betraying us, and I shall tell him as much to his face. Call a cabinet meeting at 8 p.m."

He would then announce a change of government. Peyrouton would have Laval arrested, making sure that he wasn't executed. After having complimented Laval for his work, and promising to follow him to Paris, he finally decided to fire him and have him placed under arrest.

Regaining his military commander's voice, Pétain ordered General Laure, who was always ready to carry out any drudgery, to "...draft a letter to Hitler. Say that I am very touched by his thought of bringing back the remains but that regretfully I cannot go to Paris and that I can no longer use the services of Mr. Laval. As for you Bouthillier, prepare the necessary paperwork."

"It will be very simple, Marshal: a new constitutional act withdrawing any rights to succession previously given to Laval, and two decrees to restructure the government. I shall bring them to you in half an hour."

General Laure who hadn't been told any of the details of the conspiracy took the opportunity to give du Moulin the draft of the letter to Hitler. Instructions were then given to Colonel Georges Groussard, a bald man who wore a monocle and looked like Eric von Stroheim. A former deputy commandant of the St. Cyr military academy, he was the founder and head of the G.P. or "Groupes de Protection," a special police force made up of very loyal elements who were well armed, motorized and willing to take on any assignment. Many of them were either former Cagoulards[99] street toughs; none of them would qualify as choir boys. They happened to be headquartered in the former Masonic lodge at Vichy. That night Groussard was to make sure that the Hotel du Parc was under complete control. Once his co-conspirators had departed Peyrouton was alone with Pétain who said:

"Minister, have you given any thought as to what might happen to you or to me? They could very well shoot us! I'm an old man but you are a young man."

"Everything will be just fine, Marshal."

In the meantime Alibert, seeking divine protection, had taken refuge in the Saint-Louis church while Pétain who was not a religious man remained alone possibly thinking about the Aiglon.

Peyrouton ordered that Laval's carriage be blocked at the Vichy railroad station. Darlan ordered that an officer in the Admiralty should prepare for security measures. As Admiral Le Luc asked for the reasons, Darlan, who was concerned about secrecy, gave him a curt answer: "None of your business." Just like the "pasha" (or captain) on board ship never reveals his intentions before taking action.

---

99 The "cagoulards" or "hooded ones" were the members of a secret society known as the "Cagoule," whose intent it was to overthrow the Third Republic and replace it with a dictatorial fascist-type regime. The plot was uncovered and dismantled in 1937.

At 6 p.m. the customary cabinet meeting took place to discuss the Labor Charter and a short remark was made about the Marshal's departure for Paris. At 7 p.m. while the ministers took a break, Bouthillier and Peyrouton went to the Casino to check on the preparations effected by the policemen and to make sure that every express and local train would skip the Vichy station. Baudoin returned to see Pétain in reality to keep an eye on him, while du Moulin was writing on his tiny table the draft of the letter to Hitler.

As he later wrote:

I imagined the small tomb of the Aiglon in Vienna's Kaisergruft. I try to find the best words to describe the emotions the French people would have at the return of the King of Rome, with images of 1811, Victor Hugo, the dome of the Invalides, the shadow of Metternich, the Emperor's porphyry sarcophagus and the voice of Sarah Bernhardt. But how could I make the transition from the Aiglon to Laval? How could one say in the same letter that he was so extremely grateful and not at all sorry about the daring steps he was taking? The commonly used official language doesn't lend itself to such wild acrobatics. I rewrote one draft after another. Time passed. Suddenly the door opens and it's none other than Laval coming into my office. He looks worried:

"What is this cabinet meeting all about? It wasn't discussed when we met before…"

I play dumb as best I can.

"It must be about the trip, Mr. President."

"What trip?"

"Well, the trip to Paris! You know the Marshal. He notices that the ministers are unhappy to have him travel alone. He wants to tell them himself."

"Whose idea was it?"

"I don't know, the Marshal's I assume"

"All this doesn't sound clear to me at all. Alibert must be behind it."

Laval was fidgeting nervously then asked "What are you writing?"

Du Moulin was petrified. It was the letter to Hitler that his secretary had just typed on the old vanity table that shook on its thin legs. It was a first draft, and du Moulin was caught red handed like a high school kid busy cheating, but fortunately the first page only contained the introduction and the Marshal's thanks. Sliding the other pages under his blotter du Moulin handed Laval the first page who glanced at the paper.

"Not bad," said the deputy prime minister, who recommended that the conclusion to the letter include such words as "sentiments of the highest regard."

Novelist Cecil Saint Laurent used the episode in his novel *Clotilde.*[100]

Laval now playing the role of the angry predator muttered as he lit another cigarette.

"What idiots! And to think that we are trying to rebuild France with people of that caliber!"

But du Moulin went on:

Between the sad fate of the Duke of Reichstadt—he wrote for Pétain—a prisoner of his own family and the cruel destiny of France exiled in her own country by the misfortunes of war, history will draw a moving analogy... Happy or wounded, triumphant or defeated France bows faithfully to those who over the centuries were the creators of her glory...

---

100. Cecil Saint-Laurent (real name Jacques Laurent) was a prolific author of popular adventure fiction. *Clotilde* is one of the best known of this kind.

Then at the same time since the arrest of Déat had also been decided, Alibert's chief of staff Font-Réaux phoned General La Laurencie and used the code words:

"The Marshal's wife has reached the demarcation line." But the general had forgotten the code words and really thought Mrs. Pétain was arriving with no one to welcome her. He lost his composure:

"You make endless mistakes! So the Marshal's wife now in limbo at the demarcation line since 5 p.m. It is now 8 p.m. and I have no idea as to when I can help out…You will please tell her that I am not the one responsible for such a mistake!"

"But general," replied Font-Réaux, "you haven't understood what I just said…"

"What do you mean I didn't understand! I am neither deaf nor senile!"

As he hung up the receiver he tried to reach General von Stulpnagel and failed. But a second phone call from Vichy had General Laure on the line shouting.

"Code words, code words!"

La LaurencieFornel needed a few more minutes to sort things out. He phoned Vichy back and yelled:

"I've got it!"

Laure then said:

"Immediate execution."

At 8 p.m. Laval entered the lobby of the hotel and went to the cabinet room where most of the ministers were already waiting, all of them standing up and answering his questions with feigned ignorance. Then Marshal Pétain arrived accompanied by Baudoin and his secretary general Admiral Fernet—there were admirals everywhere at Vichy—but he didn't sit down. Very pale, with a stern look in his eyes, the Marshal used the firm voice he was known to have when he imparted orders to the troops. It was a device to hide his natural shyness:

"I have decided to restructure the government. I ask each one of you to sign this letter of resignation."

In the autocratic form of government that Vichy had become, Pétain had already made similar authoritarian changes in personnel, which were thoroughly different from the custom of the Third Republic. Laval was not surprised that he had not been consulted and thought the true objective was simply to get rid of René Belin, the minister of labor. He therefore signed, unaware that he was automatically excluding himself from politics for some sixteen months.

The Marshal grabbed the piece of paper and returned upstairs to his office.

As Mallet wrote:

"That was when Laval began to feel uncomfortable and looking somber he went into the lobby." Peyrouton told Baudoin there was nothing to worry about: the hotel was surrounded by soldiers, there were policemen inside and the telephone lines had been cut.

"A South American-style coup!" was the comment of Alfred Fabre-Luce. After a few minutes Pétain returned, looking tense. His rosy complexion had turned ashen gray.[101] Without sitting down he said:

"The resignations of Messers. Laval and Ripert are accepted."[102]

It was as if thunder had struck when Louis XIV decided to cut down Nicolas Foucquet. No cabinet minister had been dismissed so brutally since that incident and even Napoleon had

---

101. Pétain, wrote Maurice Martin du Gard, owed his rosy ivory complexion to a secret formula invented by Dr. Métretrel's father who had refused to sell to Elizabeth Arden but had passed it along to his son.

102. Laval had wanted to dismiss Ripert for some time never imagining that they would both be condemned to leave together. But no one around the table took any interest in Ripert who wasn't present.

used a certain modicum of elegance in firing Talleyrand or Fouché. Laval on the other hand had never experienced such a humiliating insult in his long political career.

As Henri Amouroux described the scene:

Their closed faces masked their internal jubilation as all the ministers had abandoned him.

Alfred Mallet recounted that Pierre Laval:

Standing up like everyone else he grabbed the back of his chair like a peasant handling his plough, he arched his shoulders like an animal ready to pounce, his skin color suddenly turning darker. He looked around and with a raspy voice addressed the statue of the Commander facing him:

"What's wrong Marshal? You saw me earlier this afternoon and said nothing."

"This afternoon I was still hesitating, now it's done. The newspapers paid for by Abetz are approving your policies, going even further and they attack my orders."

"There's nothing I can do about that. Those newsmen are not obeying my orders. One must get used to being criticized by the press."

The old man unable to improvise as well as his opponent didn't look good in the art of debate that Laval had mastered to perfection. Pétain couldn't accuse Laval of collusion with the Germans since at the same time he was writing to Hitler that France's policies were not changing. He could only make statements without giving the real reasons and relying on formal explanations.

"I have no idea of what you are doing in Paris. Every time you go there I wonder what other disaster your travels will bring us."

Mallet went on:

There again the minister who had been forced to resign could easily defend himself, he had his own way of working, only the results counted. He had never withheld an explanation to Pétain personally but was wary of some of the ministers.

The counter attack was to have some effect: the Marshal was used to fighting defensive battles. He was expecting to be outflanked and took some time saying simply in a low but clear voice: "You have lost my confidence! You have lost my confidence!"

Laval had one more point: the constitutional acts were a single indivisible block.

"But you have named me your successor and I still am."

"Article 4 has just been cancelled," replied Pétain calmly. He marked a point. Alibert had already had typed a new version of that text.[103] One hundred and eight years after his death, Napoleon's rightful successor had defeated the heir apparent of Marshal Pétain. As Henri Amouroux commented:

"For the first time since May 1940 the 'blitzkrieg' had come from the French side."

Until then Laval listened leaning more and more heavily on the back of the chair. Then he stood up looking straight at the Marshal and with a slow quivering voice concluded:

---

103. According to legal experts all the "constitutional acts" signed by Pétain on July 11, 1940, were cancelled or hadn't legally taken place since they went beyond the powers given to the National Assembly. The Marshal had a special interest in the article that gave him the incredible privilege that went far beyond the provisions of constitutional law to designate his own successor. After many different changes of government that article underwent several variations during Pétain's reign.

"I have only been thinking in the interests of France. I hope Marshal that your various contradictory decisions will not harm my country too much."

The possessive he always used when he said "my country" and not "the country" or "our country" was always irritating to his adversaries. On that day the expression irritated them one last time. However it was only to last a relatively short while…

Laval looked over all the ministers. The more cynical ones had trouble hiding their jubilation; others, understanding the intensity of the moment, were serious and worried. The instant passed and the one of the most dramatic cabinet meetings in history had lasted only some fifteen minutes. The deed was done and Dr. Jekyll had momentarily defeated Mr. Hyde. But Mr. Hyde always comes back.

"You will not refuse to shake hands?" asked Laval.

The Marshal extended his hand to his former successor. The King of Italy did the same to Mussolini a few seconds before having him arrested. Then according to Albert Mallet:

After Laval left the Marshal thanked the ministers: "Gentlemen you have given me support by your presence!" It took some doing, obviously. Other famous dismissals in French history are well known. King Louis XV only needed a short note to fire Choiseul. Chautemps preferred to summon Dalimier and ask for his resignation. Never had the dismissal of a minister been so solemnly aggressive or had that kind of publicity…

Everyone sensed that the moment had historical dimensions. Did anyone think of the shadow of the young man in his white uniform?

Darlan immediately disappeared to go to the movies and made sure that the fact be known.[104] Laval, enraged and destroyed, went to his office after failing in an attempt to see the Marshal. Laure was standing guard and stopped him. The former deputy prime minister then called Châteldon but the phone line was cut. However the policemen had forgotten about the line to one of his assistants and he was able to inform his wife and daughter that he would return that evening. Then with his faithful agent Brinon he went to the restaurant in the hotel called the *Chantecler*. A newsman who saw them wrote: "He was composed but his wrist was shaking slightly when he smoked."

One can only imagine the dinner conversation the two men had, both of them bitter and reeling from a monumental defeat that had crushed them both. Laval who boasted about the fact that he had "hoodwinked" Hitler had just been had by an aging soldier he despised and whom he called a glorious nonentity. Laval was unable to grasp that what Pétain, a master of indirection, wanted most was to hang on to his power. And in this he played his cards like a master. It was no accident that the Germans referred to the Marshal as "der alte Fuchs" the old fox.

It was the only victory that Napoleon II could claim one hundred eight years after his death.

---

104. On January 10 the Admiral would dare say to J. Benoist-Méchin: "I didn't know what was being hatched. Nobody asked me. That evening I quietly went to the movies and found out about Laval's arrest only the following morning."

6.

Aftermath

As General de Gaulle said in very different circumstances: "You didn't even have to seize power but simply pick it up." Pétain immediately appointed Pierre-Étienne Flandin as foreign minister and addressed the nation at 8:30 p.m.:

Frenchmen,

I have just made a decision that I know is in the best interests of the country.

Mr. Pierre Laval is no longer part of the government.

Mr. Pierre-Étienne Flandin has been given the ministry of foreign affairs.

Constitutional act no. 4 naming my successor is cancelled.

I have reached this decision for serious reasons of internal policy. In no way does it affect our relations with Germany.

I remain in full charge. The National Revolution shall go on.[105]

Since the *Journal Officiel* was already published by 5 p.m. Vichy got the news one day earlier.

At 8 p.m. Laval returned to his office with an increasingly despondent Brinon in tow. He would later write: "I began gathering my papers; I have a habit of leaving ministries only to come back again. I therefore know when you have to pack your boxes and I did." A superstitious man, he realized that the matter had taken place on Friday the 13th.

Things could have ended there and the arrest of Laval could have taken place discreetly but Alibert—"who could teach law but not much else," as M. Martin du Gard wrote—always over-excited, decided to call Groussard and ask him to "get tough." The G.P.s, wearing their leather helmets and jackets, white gloves and machine gun strapped to their shoulder, barged into the hotel through the left staircase and began pushing back the guests, opening some doors, and shutting others and searching the entire second floor. Laval understood that this coup was meant for him and he desperately tried to meet with Pétain. "The head of state is sleeping" was the only answer he received.

But some people had just seen the elevator go up with a jocular Marshal Pétain wearing his brand new suit and holding a pretty young lady in a red bodice very close to him. When he felt in the mood to speak in confidence he would often say: "I loved two things in my life, making love and the infantry."

---

105. Later on in order to avoid poisoning his relationship with Laval he decided not to publish this text in the edition of his *Messages* of which he was very proud. He discovered late in life that he enjoyed being a successful author even though other people had actually done the writing. In fact the only real gripe he had against de Gaulle concerned an authorship dispute between them about the book, *La France et son armée*. Pétain's protests to Hitler regarding armistice violations—the de facto annexation of Alsace-Lorraine by Germany—were also omitted from the book.

After victory in battle the Marshal turned to women, the timeless reward for the victorious general. Laval summoned du Moulin.

"What's going on? My chauffeur has just been arrested. My car has been taken by the police with all my documents. One of my secretaries is locked in her room. This all looks like a provocation. Are they going to throw me in jail?"

"Mr. President you understand that the Marshal…"

"But what is he doing now?"

"He's sleeping."

"Ah! Sleeping is he. Well go wake him up. Tell him they are going to arrest me, they are going over his head, they are trampling on his orders. Go!"

Du Moulin went up one floor. Pétain was in his bathrobe unable to sleep—the excitement had been too great—and said

"So he's unhappy?"

"One would have to be for much less, Marshal."

"Well too bad, he got what he deserves. Tell him I'm asleep and try to gain time. It should be all over by 11 p.m."

Du Moulin returned downstairs to an increasingly excited Laval.

"I tell you they're going to string me up! And I have no way of defending myself (he took a pen knife out of his pocket). Those bastards!"

Midnight. The former deputy prime minister was still shuffling papers and getting ready to go to the station to board the train to Paris when Mondanel, the head of the Sûreté appeared in his dark overcoat.

"Mr. President I have orders to place you under arrest."

"Show me your warrant; you must have one."

Mondanel took the paper out of his wallet.

"So I see: it's signed by Peyrouton. Since when does the minister of the interior have the right to arrest the deputy prime minister?"

"Mr. President, he is acting under orders of the Marshal."

"That's not written here. I demand a confirmation on the part of Marshal Pétain."

Laval was splitting hairs as usual: he no longer was deputy prime minister and the minister of the interior could in fact have him arrested just like any other Frenchman. The head of the Sûreté didn't dare answer and sent an emissary to the floor directly above. General Laure confirmed that the arrest had been decided by Marshal Pétain himself. As Napoleon said to Marshal Soult at Austerlitz.

"Marshal, you have covered yourself with glory."

The deputy prime minister under arrest appeared in the hotel lobby flanked by two policemen: he had only been spared the shame of having to wear handcuffs. They went out into the ice-cold night where there were policemen everywhere. Escorted by the two police inspectors Laval left in his own car. In his twenty-year political career, he had experienced many an honor guard but never this intrusive escort due a perpetrator.

During the ride, he was able to think about his actions and assess his position. Devoid of any interest in history, it didn't occur to Laval to compare his fate to that of General Malet [106] when he failed in his plot against Napoleon. He may have thought back to Caillaux whom Clemenceau had prosecuted for going too far in his dealings with the Kaiser's Germany, then also France's enemy. Pétain, however, was no Clemenceau but Laval no doubt had counted that fact once too often.

Laval felt very uneasy as they drove through the forest: were they about to kill him just as it would happen later to Mandel and Jean Zay? [107] The Vichy government at that time in 1940 was

---

106. General Malet attempted a military coup to overthrow Napoleon but failed.

107. Both Georges Mandel and Jean Zay, two former ministers and members of parliament, were Jewish and were murdered by the French collaborationist Milice in 1944.

still behaving in a rather civilized manner. Laval began to feel better as soon as he recognized the first houses that were part of his village and his own home. What he called his "château" was actually just a big country house with a pointed roof, the largest in the region. It was now surrounded by two companies of motorized policemen.

The Deputy Prime Minister had been dismissed like a servant and would have the luxury of meditating at length on the Marshal's ingratitude since he owed his rise to power to Pierre Laval. The house arrest and isolation by an unusually large security detail showed how fearful the perpetrators were of the former designated successor to the Head of State.

At the same time on the second floor of the hotel, the G.P.s (the special police "Groupes de Protection") were in complete control and had no hesitation in barging into the halls and lounges filled with the rather miserable gifts that had been sent to the Marshal. The staff members who worked closely with Laval had been locked in their rooms with a policeman at the door or even inside their room that also served as an office. "You can imagine the complete surprise of those couples who had to spend the night under the watchful eye of an armed guard." as du Moulin noted, walking through the halls looking official he was promptly stopped by a guard:

"But," he said with his usual self-importance, "I am from the floor above. I am the Marshal's cabinet director…"

"That's not written on your nose, my friend…," answered the policeman.

Brinon had left his pajamas in a bag in Laval's car that had gone off to Châteldon and had to spend the night wearing his gold braided uniform dozing off on an armchair in his wife's room. It was something that hadn't happened to him in a long time. The telephone was cut and he preferred not to speak anyway for fear of wiretaps. His son Bernard Ullman was also there and described Brinon as "silent, somber and looking dejected." At some point the "marquise" in her bathrobe and overexcited as usual opened the door and dashed into the hallway:

"They want to murder my husband!"

Brinon, exasperated pushed her back inside rather rudely. They were freed the following day and Brinon left a bit crumpled as he told his wife.

"My dear I shall return to Paris this evening to try and patch things up."

His son-in-law wrote that he slammed the door as he left.

No doubt someone had forgotten to cut one more telephone line because a phone began ringing in an office that night. It was the Vichy railroad station asking what they should do with Laval's private carriage: the midnight train was late and the travelers were unaware that they were in the midst of a coup d'état and were getting impatient. Railroad officials didn't know what to answer. Five minutes later there was another phone call. A G.P. with a gun in hand answered:

"This is the stationmaster."

"I don't like fancy jokes," said the cop out of his depth.

Then there was the most suggestive touch: the secretaries were told to undress and get into bed but leave their doors open. They should have no fear for their virtue with so many people milling around the hotel. The commotion also made it possible to scare off the long term customers who wanted to remain in the establishment.

After the crisis some of Laval's staff were held under guard for five days and one of them was sent to prison for three months.

In some ways Laval's dismissal prompted by the return of Napoleon II is very much akin to the "rather rough police action" as the Duke of Morny described the coup d'état of Louis Napoléon Bonaparte some eighty-nine years earlier when he grabbed the throne that his first cousin, the son of Napoleon had lost.

At around 6:30 a.m. on Saturday, December 14, it was still pitch black in Paris since the city was forced to live on Berlin time. Marcel Déat was yanked out of bed in his pajamas by the head of the municipal police who showed him a piece of school notebook paper where General La Laurencie had written in block letters:

"On orders from Marshal Pétain you shall arrest Monsieur Marcel Déat."

The politician had only one reaction: "Have you informed the German ambassador?" Then he prepared his things without any complaints and asked his wife to inform the occupation authorities. He spent the whole morning at the police Préfecture and was set free at noon. Mrs. Déat managed to reach one of Abetz's assistants who despite the precautions taken at Vichy had been informed of Laval's arrest that same night.

Without a doubt Otto Abetz was the one German most affected by the unfolding events.

"I wanted to offer France a bouquet of violets but France just trampled it" he said.

He had staked his political career on his relationship with Laval, recommending that Pétain be moved to Versailles but now suddenly Abetz was running the risk of being dismissed, by-passed and perhaps even worse, arrested. The return of the Aiglon that was his pet project turned into a very unlucky under-taking: would he be ordered back to a desk at the Wilhelmstrasse or to the war front in Libya instead? Early that morning he summoned General La Laurencie to the embassy in the rue de Lille that looked more like "some kind of animal farm." Abetz was furious and worried: furious because he had to cancel the trips planned for Hitler and Göring since Pétain would not show up and worried because of the consequences these events would have on his own career.

The poor general recalled: "I was completely overtaken by events. I was immediately shown in to see Mr. Abetz and his two councilors Messers. Achenbach and Schleier. The man I was facing as I walked in was literally foaming with rage. Abetz was pacing up and down the room, gesticulating in an odd way, flashing his blood shot eyes at me... He was like an animal out of control..."

Gesticulating and yelling just like Hitler, Abetz insulted La Laurencie as every drop of his celebrated Francophilia vanished.

"I don't need to listen to you... You have arrested Monsieur Déat. I order you to free him within the hour..."

The general was a bit dense but kept his sense of honor:

"I arrested him under orders from my government."

"I order that you free him."

"I only follow the orders of my government."

"If Monsieur Déat is not freed immediately, I shall take you hostage..."

"Threats have never frightened me," replied the general.

Not knowing how to answer, Abetz banged his fist on his desk in frustration and left the room.

The inimitable La Laurencie ended the meeting.

"Gentlemen, I feel I can only take my leave, and must note that diplomatic conversations have taken an unusual twist today."

He then phoned Vichy, unaware of Laval's demise when he described the anger displayed by Abetz. "I understand less and less." he ended up saying.

By the end of the morning Abetz informed Vichy through La Laurencie of his requests.

"The government of the Reich must inform the Head of State that it demands that Monsieur Marcel Déat be set free immediately; that a direct phone line be established between Monsieur de Brinon and the rue de Lille. That the government will not arrest any other political figures; and requires that the embassy be informed on what basis the French government thinks it has the right to cancel constitutional decrees."

(Amazingly enough, Nazi Germany dared mention the existence of a constitution…)

The atmosphere was tense since the Germans had moved armored vehicles to certain segments of the demarcation line. The Marshal called in a few ministers and drafted an answer meant to gain time. He accepted the first two demands and by passed the third by saying he had no intention of arresting anyone while he ignored the fourth demand which was equivalent to rejecting it as being contrary to national sovereignty—or at least what was left of it. The answer was phoned in to Paris on December 14 at twelve thirty. Déat was immediately freed and had a champagne lunch with his wife. The replies had gone through La Laurencie who remained completely in the dark:

"Can you give me more explanations?" he pleaded with Vichy.

"Not for the moment. But what do they think about Uncle Pierre in Paris?"

"Nothing" answered the general who wondered whose uncle that was.

Brinon however had managed to call Abetz who offered a rogue explanation:

"The government of the Reich–meaning Ribbentrop whom Pétain referred to as 'the traveling imitation-champagne sales-man,'—must inform the Head of the French State that the remains of the Duke of Reichstadt will not be handed over to General La LaurencieFornel —that no one seemed to like that much—and hopes that the Marshal and President Laval will attend the ceremony."

Encouraged and egged on, Pétain, with renewed resolve, appointed the members of the official delegation to attend the ceremony. There was no chance of sending Flandin whom the

Germans had not yet and never would recognize; Darlan who rested on his reputation as an undefeated leader would represent the government and General Laure would represent the Marshal himself: the admiral had five stars, and the general three making a strange number to stand in for the seven stars of a Marshal of France.

The Paris newspapers, obeying the orders of the occupation authorities, said nothing about these changes which were not even mentioned in *L'Illustration*. The entire northern portion of France had no knowledge that Laval was out of power. At Châteldon, defeated by the shadow of Napoleon II, he muttered: "I have been had like a choir boy."

The pro-de Gaulle radio in London was to comment: "Tempest in a bottle of Vichy water."

That evening in Paris the ceremony was to begin deprived of the significance that Hitler intended it to have.

7.

A Stormy Return

Alas! Where are the eagles and the proud emblems
That were to preside over the Aiglon's return
Where are the flags flapping for the blond child?
The shadow around this shadow created the
    anathema.

Monique Defrane
L'Autre retour des cendres[108]

On the morning of December 15 the atmosphere at Vichy remained tense. Bouthillier wrote: "The Marshal was asking himself aloud "Did we do the right thing? What will come out of all this?" Darlan and Laure left the Hotel du Parc at 3 p.m. to get on the Paris train with their aides de camp—a rather

---

108. From a poem written in 1940 in Grenoble by a young woman student, Monique Defrane, who was upset by this example of collaboration. The entire poem was published by its author in a collection of her works, *Du cyprès à l'olivier* (Paris, Gallimard, 1959.)

low profile group compared to the prominent mission on board *la Belle Poule* one century before. At 8 p.m. the two envoys were in the office of General La Laurencie who finally got his complete briefing and the three of them then left together.

At 11 p.m. on December 15 the capital was under curfew and a light freezing rain mixed with snow flurries and sleet began to fall. A few Paris newsmen invited the day before were at the German embassy, the former residence of Eugene de Beauharnais, in the rue de Lille, without having been told the reason. In the vast Hall of Seasons heavily decorated with moldings, columns, palm motifs and large allegorical paintings, the Vichy officials were welcomed by Otto Abetz, looking very sour in his gray green uniform with large white lapels and Fernand de Brinon, in full diplomatic gold braided uniform. Also present was Marcel Déat who had been plucked from prison to attend the ceremonial event just a few hours earlier. A few important persons had received a permit to attend written in both languages.

Abetz, in attempting to hide his anger and his fear, informed the journalists about the return of the Aiglon and named the three men who had made the event possible: Jacques Benoist-Méchin, Fernand de Brinon and Pierre Laval. Even though, as mentioned earlier, the first had expressed his opposition, Brinon had followed orders as usual and Laval was under house arrest at Châteldon. Abetz regretted that Laval was absent without offering any explanation and made it a point to note that without him the "historic return" would have certainly not been possible—of course, Laval had nothing to do with the Duke's return. As the frustrated ambassador underlined "It is he [Laval] who created the atmosphere of collaboration and he remains the only guarantor of that policy as far as we are concerned." Most of the people in attendance didn't understand the meaning of that remark. Abetz knew what had happened at Vichy and Germany was rejecting the coup.

Abetz then made the required reference to Napoleon who, he said "Has never been closer to us, not just from a national point of view of his struggle against the reactionaries who had victimized the King of Rome, but from the European point of view since Napoleon was the one who revived the great popular movements whose modern equivalents are Italian fascism, German national-socialism, Spanish nationalism that are now also influencing France." The emperor was therefore a precursor and creator of collectivist movements that were not yet known during his time.

Fernand de Brinon answered in elegant terms and with restrained gestures. Even though he was an ambassador, he no longer held any official position since he only represented the fallen Laval. The delegate general of the French government in the occupied zone was still General La LaurencieFornel whom the Germans despised and who enjoyed little esteem in France. He had not been invited to attend. Brinon was soon to take over his job. The marquis answered emphatically, as circumstances required, without giving a reason for Laval's absence, saying that the deputy prime minister wanted to be present to receive the Führer's gift. "A gesture coming from a very great leader and a giant of a man as the collaboration between the two countries is about to enter a critical phase." Brinon then returned to the Faucigny-Lucinge residence on the elegant Avenue Foch that he had requisitioned for himself.

The Germans had spent the entire day at the Invalides preparing for the ceremony. The cannons of the "triumphal battery" had been removed from the terrace of the parade ground and all evening mortuary wreaths were brought over one after the other and lined up in the first winter snow just outside the Dôme church. It was at that moment that the episode recounted by Anne Muratori-Philip took place.

In a small low building in between two courtyards (it no longer exists after the rebuilding of the Jardin de l'Intendant) lived the Morins. The Mr. Morin was a veteran of the First World War employed by the "Office national des combatants," a veteran's association headquartered in the building while his wife was a volunteer for historical monuments. The arrival of the wreaths attracted their attention, especially the largest one adorned with a swastika made of posies and the inscription *From Chancellor Hitler to the Duke of Reichstadt.*

The scene prompted the total outrage of the Morin family. Before the torchlights were lit, Denise Morin wearing her felt slippers on the snow grabbed the obscene wreath and dragged it into her house where it was promptly chopped up and stuffed into the family furnace. That night her husband emptied out the ashes and retrieved the burnt out iron frame that he buried at the foot of a tree.

Meanwhile in Vienna the crypt of the Capuchins was opened late on the morning of Thursday December 12.[109] The Aiglon's sarcophagus had been in the crypt for one hundred and eight years, much longer than Napoleon's body remained at Saint Helena before being returned. A special honor guard presented arms and a thick crowd walked behind the casket to the station where a special train with all curtains drawn was ready to leave. The casket was placed in a carriage that had been turned into a mourning chapel and the train left at slow speed in the direction of Paris. It took the same glorious route in the opposite direction that Napoleon had traveled twice as a conqueror. The train reached the Gare de l'Est on Saturday the 14th. Either because of forgetfulness or simple negligence, the Prince's heart and insides remained in Vienna where they had been placed one hundred and eight years before.

---

109. Thanks to the information provided by the Provincial head of the Capuchins of Vienna, since the Anschluss the Habsbourg family had lost all its rights to the crypt of the Capuchins that was managed by the Capuchin order. A few days before the transfer, the Gestapo informed the Capuchins of Hitler's decision and that the extraction of the casket was to take very quickly. There are no documents regarding the matter in the Capuchin archives.

A projector lit up the casket surrounded by Austrian fir trees, the casket was covered with a black cloth emblazoned with a cross decorated with clover leaf branches. A red and gold crest carried the Prince's ducal coat of arms. One hundred twenty six years after leaving Paris, the Aiglon had returned. The Austrians had taken him away as a hostage and the Germans were returning him to serve their political purpose and their glory: in fact it was just another form of hostage taking.

On the tracks in front of a small group of Frenchmen, the doors slid open throwing off some of the snow accumulated during the trip. Two German soldiers in their green uniforms stood at attention on either side of the open door. A German honor guard in helmets and bearing arms, with some of the men carrying torches, marched on the platform. The officers formed a circle in front of the carriage. Twenty-four men were required to carry the bronze sarcophagus that weighed eight hundred kilos and place it with a black funeral draping on the gun carriage. The carriage was hitched up to an armored track vehicle in front of the station flanked by a light artillery battery. Then with light snow flurries, and without any French soldiers, the funeral convoy crossed a deserted Paris in a cold, frosty silence.

As Anne Muratori-Philip wrote:

"An icy breeze shot through the sorcerer's apprentices of that night. The Führer's brainchild resembled the naked trees covered with ice as the snow kept falling in drifts. The flakes rested on the black cloth covering the casket before melting like silver tears."

The weather resembled the retreat from Russia rather than the sunny coronation of the Emperor.

"A clandestine tragedy, under torchlight in an angry atmosphere of consternation and mourning,"

Wrote Benoist-Méchin. Even in his birthplace and capital, Napoleon II remained a prisoner.

Behind the sad and naked gun carriage there was no one to accompany the Aiglon during his final journey: not a single member of the two families, nor any civilian or military personality, no one was present to remember the unhappy prince after his death. In the dark and deserted streets where only a few windows were barely opened from time to time because of the noise, motorcycle riders preceded the funeral march made up of six heavy field cannon followed by a few cars. The slow convoy of green uniforms escorting a body dressed in a white uniform marched down the boulevards de Strasbourg and Sébastopol. It passed in front of the Châtelet Column that celebrates Napoleon's victories, touched the shadow of the Tuileries palace where the child king was born, past the water's edge terrace on the banks of the Seine where in childhood he was taken in a small carriage drawn by a few sheep trained by Franconi. He continued all the way to the esplanade using the same itinerary as Napoleon's funeral march a century before but this time in a dark and damp silence compared to the wild enthusiasm that had accompanied the return of his father's coffin. The France of 1940 and the Empire of Napoleon had both gone down in defeat.

Napoleon's cortège had entered the Invalides through the northern honor court; his son's circled the building and came directly to the door of the Dôme church using the same itinerary as Louis XIV to the place Vauban past the statues of marshals Galliéni and Fayolle that were being ignored on this occasion. On the small Place Denys-Cochin what remained of the monument to General Mangin could still be seen. The Germans had torn down the statue a few weeks before.[110]

---

110. While the Germans had not touched the monuments of the leaders of the First World War, they exceptionally destroyed the one to General Mangin on June 27, 1940, because he was in command of colonial troops and had been in favor of the independence of the Rhineland. The head of the mutilated statue is in the Army museum. See G. Poisson's article, "Le sort des

Two hundred Republican guards in formal dress uniform with ceremonial helmets formed a double row in the wide court-yard in front of the Dôme. Each man was holding a torch of sparkling resin that glowed in the dark. As Anne Muratori-Philip described it:

"The Dôme took on a reddish color under the moving lights and the desperate contortions of the shadows against the front of the church."

A Wagnerian spectacle as the French and German commentators described it in their identical contrived style.

The officials and a few guests had been waiting for one hour behind the gates in the snow covered courtyard: it was just as cold as one century before. Admiral Darlan in his navy blue uniform studded with stars on his sleeves; Generals Laure and La Laurencie with their gold embroidered képis stood in front, followed by a number of shadows among them Abel Bonnard soon to become a Vichy government minister but already known to favor the collaboration policy; Professor and polemical journalist Marcel Déat who seemed to ignore Darlan's presence; Charles Trochu vice president of the Paris municipal council; Sacha Guitry the famous actor and film director who could always be counted on to attend any kind of show; Elvire Popesco another actress who also happened to be present; right-wing writers Bernard Faÿ, and René Benjamin; the Count and Countess de Chambrun, the direct descent of the Marquis de Lafayette while his wife was the daughter of Pierre Laval, Josée.

Drieu La Rochelle left an authentic tableau of his impressions. Some rather uncharitable historians would later tease André Castelot about his attending the event that day but he did mention the fact in his book about the Aiglon.[111] General

---

statues de bronze parisiennes sous l'occupation allemande," in *Paris et l'Île de France*, 1998.

111. Popular French historian André Castelot was the son of Gabrielle Stroms known as Castelot, the mistress and assistant to Alphonse de

Mariaux, a wounded veteran and the governor of the Invalides, was also present in his little carriage, among the rest of the small crowd. General La Laurencie was constantly pulling up his white gloves to strike a pose while other German embassy personnel remained outside the gates.

The door to the Dôme church was wide open to welcome the visitors. From their pedestals on either side, the statues of Saint Louis and Charlemagne were waiting for the representative of the Napoleonic dynasty, the fourth in France's royal and imperial history. Inside the church the Republican Guards were lined up on both sides up to the main altar forming a line of sentries around the Tomb of the Emperor awaiting the son that had been taken away from him at age three. A large projector placed behind the altar, sent a beam of light toward the vaulted ceiling enhancing the twisted columns that held up the canopy.

Messengers announced the arrival of the funeral cortège at one twenty. Darlan and Laure came up to the wide open gates. Preceded by whistles a few cars stopped outside, Otto Abetz emerged from one of them quickly followed by General Otto von Stulpnagel, the military governor of Paris and the prototype of the brutal and pitiless Junker who would acquire an awful reputation during the occupation. He would later commit suicide in his cell at the Cherche-Midi prison in 1948.

Perhaps in order to signal that he was the welcoming host in his own domain, Darlan stepped forward toward the handsome German ambassador. At the same moment behind the Admiral in the Place Vauban orders were being shouted in German and shadowy figures were making haste. Two minutes later, announced by the sounds of bugles, the heavy carriage and its caisson stopped in front of the gates. Some men took their hats off while others saluted militarily; Brinon avoided giving the Nazi salute even though he would do so copiously later on; the

---

Châteaubriant and a pro-Hitler writer herself. See Gilbert Joseph, *Fernand de Brinon.*

helmeted sentries stood at attention under the snow flakes and presented arms.

During this aborted ceremony that had lost its initial meaning, there was nothing of the pageantry of the Prince of Joinville presenting himself to his father, King Louis-Philippe with his sword in hand.[112] But this was no time for eloquence and even less for comparisons. In 1840 the King himself had welcomed the casket. In 1940 Joinville was replaced by a foreign enemy ambassador, a kind of Hudson Lowe character in a sense.[113] Still smarting from his disappointment, Abetz could only tell Darlan:

"As the bronze casket crosses the gates of the Invalides the remains of the Duke of Reichstadt become French once again and shall forever rest on French soil."

The Admiral thanked him with a few words, the subject was delicate and the situation even more tense; furthermore Darlan had no gift of oratory:

"I thank you for returning the son of our Emperor to us."

And he saluted in a gesture he was to repeat many times in later months in front of friends and enemies. His detractors called him "the bowing admiral." Just as Joinville had accompanied Napoleon to the Invalides, Darlan was on hand to welcome the Aiglon but as a sailor he was probably not as good at it as the prince. Oddly enough the event was the beginning of the admiral's rise to power. The anti-Laval conspirators had done all the dirty work and Darlan would soon accumulate far more power than his predecessor ever had. The admiral went actually much further into collaboration with nazi Germany than Laval had envisioned at that point. But once he proved unable of saving his fleet, the admiral resigned without being asked. Two

---

112 François d'Orléans, Prince de Joinville (1818–1900), was the third son of King Louis-Philippe.
113 Hudson Lowe (1769–1844), British general who is remembered as Napoleon's jailer at Saint Helena.

years later, on December 24, 1942, he would be assassinated in obscure circumstances in Algiers. The sailor who welcomed back Napoleon II was far less successful than those who served his father.

Some twenty German soldiers wearing helmets took hold of the long and narrow casket designed for a tall and thin body and placed it on a podium in front of the church. Following orders the soldiers saluted, turned about-face and marched back to the gates as they disappeared into the night. For a few moments the casket stood alone, surrounded by the silence of "an imposing grandeur," as Abetz was to write later despite his personal bitterness. Laval was absent and unable to attend otherwise he could have knelt in tears at the foot of the casket like so many veterans who welcomed Napoleon in 1840. That was clearly something that was not part of Laval's character.

There was also no interest in opening the casket for an unforgettable view as it happened at Saint Helena in 1840. No one would ever know after one hundred eight years what the body of the Aiglon looked like.[114]

Breaking the silence a trumpet sounded "Aux champs"—the French funeral tune—that broke the silence. Then a different order was shouted in French: fifteen Republican Guards wearing shako helmets came up to the bronze casket lifting it with its wooden supports and fighting the weight and the snow just as one hundred years before the sailors of *La Belle Poule* had carried the father's casket. In the newspaper style of those years we quote from the article by Robert de Beauplan in *L'Illustration*:

"It was an unforgettable moment and perhaps a poet could best express it… The snow was falling harder; somewhere to the right one could hear a muffled and melancholy roll of the drums; in front there was a man standing rigidly at attention who looked

---

114. In 1932, for the hundredth anniversary of the death of Napoleon II, Dr. Otto Ernst stated that given the care taken in preparing the prince for burial had there been an exhumation of the body it would likely be intact.

ready to burst from the tension of every muscle, with his hat off and his white hair soon to be covered with snow, he cried in silence: nothing was missing to the scene, not even the image of that anonymous man, the retired soldier of Napoleon coming back to life to welcome his Emperor's son. From now on the Duke of Reichstadt belongs only to France."

Following the casket to the muffled sounds of the drums (the same drumbeat played in honor of the Emperor on the most solemn occasions) there slowly marched with their gold braided uniforms shining in the torchlight Darlan, Laure, La Laurencie, the police prefect Langeron, the colonel in command of the Republican guard and the Minister of Supply Achard— who appeared for the first and only time on such an official occasion. Weygand was not part of the group much to Darlan's relief. The newspapers did mention the presence of a certain "Mr. Marchand" as if the faithful valet of Napoleon had returned a century later.

Inside the Dôme church filled with the sounds of the Requiem, were a few representatives of the imperial aristocracy whom Brinon had managed to bring together. The procession went around the "well of glory" as Anna de Noailles described it, where four Republican Guards stood guard at Napoleon's tomb in pink porphyry. The casket was placed on the bier at the foot of the steps leading up to the main altar. "The incense curled up in white puffs in front of a red carpet covered with imperial bees" as Anne Muratori-Philip wrote. An immense tricolor cloth dramatically enhanced by the bright light of the projector on its tarnished bronze casing all the way to the steps leading up to the altar.

Following a brief religious service, an odd midnight mass, those in attendance left quickly. Marcel Déat who doesn't seem to have observed or remembered much would write later on:

"No crowds obviously, only the press and the officials. Was this the funeral of a policy? I got back home feeling very cold but curious to witness the coming events and quite determined to do everything so that it wouldn't be what the Vichy conspirators wanted."

While he drank hot lemonade and dunked his feet in steaming water,[115] Déat took comfort at the thought that there were two kinds of Frenchmen: those that were pro-German and the "attentistes" or "wait-and-see" types and he was about to print renewed virulent attacks against the latter that had come to his mind while he was being held in prison. During the four years of German occupation as a passive and hateful spectator Déat would take the attitude of Talleyrand at the twilight of the Empire but with far less planning and refinement.

The German and French authorities took leave of each other in a cold salute. Otto Abetz was furious at having played the part of Metternich as guardian of the Aiglon as he witnessed the collapse of his scheme and had by then completely forgotten his Francophile attitude. He became roguish and almost insulting as he addressed Darlan and Laure.

"Wait at your hotel. I will have an important communication for both of you later on."

At the hotel the two men waited for some time. Then Darlan, who disliked staying up late, went to bed while the poor Laure remained awake like a sentry. Finally at four in the morning a messenger from Abetz arrived:

"It is strictly forbidden that the Vichy government mention in any way what took place on December 13th"

Laure went upstairs to wake up Darlan, who muttered:

"Handle it."

As Laure recounted:

"I got on the phone with du Moulin de la Barthète at Vichy (it had to be the morning of December 15). They told me: the newspapers are out, there's nothing we can do."

---

115. Marcel Déat, *Journal de guerre.*

The next day, Sunday December 15, under a weak sunshine, the second ceremony at the Invalides was more impressive, mostly because of the Republican Guards in full dress uniform consisting of a helmet with a chenille and red plumes, the last vestige of the uniforms of Napoleon's "Grande Armée," black tunic, white breeches, and patent leather boots. Ten guards were on either side of the casket in front of the main altar, with their sword at their side unsheathed. Four wooden eagles were placed at the corners of the bronze sarcophagus surrounded by the flags of the First Empire. Fauré's *Requiem,* conducted by concert-master Pierné, filled the space designed by Jules Hardouin-Mansart.

There were more people in attendance than the night before and the Napoleonic family was present in greater numbers which would create problems for some of its members later on. Victor, the heir to the imperial throne, the grandson of King Jérôme had to wait for the death of Leopold II to marry his daughter, Princess Clémentine of Belgium. From that late marriage was born in 1914 Prince Louis-Napoléon who joined the French foreign legion in 1939 using the assumed name of Blanchard, but remained under the law of exile banning him from living in France.

He retired to his well-known villa of Prangins in Switzerland where the Germans sent him an invitation to attend the ceremony, which he refused. Yet on that Sunday, December 15 his widowed mother, the Princesse Clémentine attended along with many more representatives of the old imperial aristocracy than the night before. There were the representative descendants of Suchet, Masséna, and Murat[116] who later joined the resistance

---

116. Louis-Gabriel Suchet, duke of Albufera and Valencia (1770–1826); André Masséna, duke of Rivoli, prince of Essling (1758–1817); Joachim Murat, King of Naples and Sicily (1767–1815).

movement, the princess of the Moskova and Koechlin-Schwartz who was far from imagining such a return eight years before.[117]

"Assembled under the German boot the descendants of the marshals and of the imperial nobility represent a Waterloo where Blücher was now named Stulpnagel since the military commander who had just ordered the execution of several freedom fighters was in attendance next to Otto Abetz," as Gilbert Joseph writes.

Abetz was also back, still smarting with fear and La Laurencie, the prefects, the director of the Légion des combattants and Xavier Vallat who would run into serious problems later on. Among the Germans, Lieutenant Heller of the Propagandastaffel who would consistently provide "help" to French writers throughout the occupation.

None of the third and fourth cousins of the Aiglon in the Habsbourg family were present, since Hitler had been born during their reign, he decided that they were to be erased from the new Germany. On the other hand at the far end of the chapel just as in the previous century, and wearing the same uniform, a few of wounded veterans of both world wars were present irrespective of whether they had survived victories or defeats.

"Incense filled the air from the depths of the crypt, rising in waves where the twisted columns of the altar became visible. A golden ray of sunlight crossed the reflection of tinted stained glass windows," as an anonymous news reporter wrote.

There were two cardinals present at the ceremony: Monsignor Suhard the Archbishop of Paris in his *cappa magna* and white bishop's miter and the tiny Monsignor Baudrillart the rector of the Catholic Institute and an academician who as of November 21 had only espoused the policy of collaboration and now dared to appear as officiating in front of Napoleon, Foch

---

117. Some of those present like the Duke of Albufera, a descendant of Suchet, were criticized by some nationalists because of their presence.

and the Aiglon. Baudrillart was to remain faithful to his opinions to his death that came early enough to spare his having to explain his choices.[118]

At the elevation, drums were rolled and bugles blared until the absolution and death march.

For a few brief moments the crowd remembered the Napoleonic glory and was able to forget the reality of a pillaged and enslaved France.

"Time had stopped inside that church....but not outside where the protocol officers were frantic: everyone was looking for the Führer's wreath!" wrote Anne Muratori-Philip. All the shuffling proved useless and Ambassador Abetz had to walk next to Darlan who was carrying a magnificent wreath wrapped in the tricolor flag and the inscription "Marshal Pétain." They walked passed the tombs of Grand Marshals Duroc and Bertrand then the bronze statues of the "Renommées" by Duret toward the tomb of porphyry where the Admiral presented his wreath. Princess Napoleon, who was standing next to him, lowered her head one last time to honor the founder of the dynasty. Brinon was also present with his traitor's face.

The invalid governor general in his little cart was perhaps thinking that his predecessor General Moncey, who a century before at the end of the ceremony for Napoleon I was lifted out of his seat and said: "Now let us go home to die."

The crowd broke up quickly because of the cold.[119]

---

118. Baudrillart wrote his daily thoughts, actions and inclinations in his notebooks. However, those referring to the occupation have not been published.

119. After some seventy-six years how many of those in attendance are still alive today (2007)? We were able to locate one through Doctor Catinat. Mr. René Deck who was very young at the time and came with his father from Hénin-Liétard but he unfortunately doesn't remember anything. (His story was published in the article by Thierry Choffat that was already cited.) The author is searching for any other surviving witnesses.

Hitler had therefore fulfilled the wish he expressed at the Invalides when he visited Paris six months before.[120] It has often been written that the Führer was seeking to gain the favor of the French people and therefore entice them into a policy of collaboration. Actually it was Vichy that had asked and literally begged for collaboration which Hitler always viewed as worthless. As he had written years earlier in *Mein Kampf,* France was not at all to be associated with Germany but rather should be its vassal; an object of exploitation and not of good relations. The gesture regarding the return of the Aiglon was not meant to impress French public opinion but was instead one of Hitler's pet projects and comparing himself to Napoleon was very much a part of his views up to the invasion of Russia. The Emperor had successfully blended Revolution and Conservatism just as Hitler mixed socialism with nationalism. Like Napoleon in France, Hitler saw himself as the reformer of the German state; he created a great army and used it to conquer half of Europe. France after successive amputations would be in a position similar to that of Prussia after the battle of Jena. Just like Napoleon, Hitler had failed to invade England and the Luftwaffe's defeat was exactly like the emperor's "Camp de Boulogne." However like Napoleon, Hitler wasn't about to give up in his attempt to defeat Great Britain which remained the enemy at war and in the propaganda war. The ceremony at the Invalides could perhaps rekindle French hostility against England, the centuries-old enemy and even the score against those Frenchmen who listened to *Radio-London.*

Pétain's rejection, and the sudden demise of Pierre Laval, had thwarted the propaganda initiative. For Hitler however

---

120. Jean de Bourgoing, author of *Le Fils de Napoléon en images,* states that the Führer had fulfilled the Prince's wish according to a letter where he asked to be buried next to his father. However, in 1832, when the Aiglon died, Napoleon's body was at Saint-Helena and there were no plans to bring it back at the time.

England wasn't the main enemy and while he decided against comparing himself to Napoleon he would follow him diligently straight into the same mistakes. The planning for *Barbarossa*[121] coincides with the Aiglon's return. Like Napoleon at Boulogne the new warlord had decided to redeploy his armies in the East because he would soon launch his assault on Russia where he was convinced he would succeed in spite of the odds. But unlike Napoleon, he never managed to take Moscow.

As for the imperial son returned to rest next to his father, was it not a way to proclaim Hitler's personal glory next to his model in a defeated and subjugated France? But then there would be no Saint-Helena for the German dictator.

There is no need in our view to turn this episode into legend, but instead let us consider it for the strange business that it turned out to be.

Count de Güell, grandee of Spain had been in contact with various European diplomats and politicians before 1939 and wrote in his *Journal d'un émigré catalan*:

"The imperial family whose current heir, Prince Napoleon a resident of Switzerland and his mother Princess Clémentine were supposed to attend the ceremony. The plan was that during the burial inside the chapel when Prince Napoleon was present, people would suddenly cry out 'Long live the Emperor!' A crowd assembled outside was to cheer the Prince and take him to the Tuileries where he would be proclaimed Emperor of the French by the people and the Paris city council.[122] Faced with such a popular demonstration the Germans would agree to a spectacular move by evacuating the occupied zone of France except for the Atlantic ports thus allowing the new Emperor to

---

121. Hitler signed Directive 21 for Operation Barbarossa on December 18, 1940.

122. Count de Güell apparently forgot that the Tuileries Palace had burned to the ground sixty years before or was the proclamation of the Third French Empire to take place in the gardens?

declare war on England. The freedom awarded to France, the memory of Saint-Helena and the high probability of military success would be enough to draw the majority of French public opinion."

It does appear that a few unrealistic individuals at the time were considering a conspiracy approved by Hitler to create a "Third French Empire." Thierry Choffat has described this strange project in detail.

We shall not dwell on the outlandish aspects of such a plan. As someone who despised all dynasties, Adolf Hitler was far from thinking of putting Prince Napoleon at the helm of a puppet state. The nighttime return of the Aiglon, far from any crowds makes the whole adventurous scenario sound even less realistic. In any case Prince Napoleon was cautious enough to skip the ceremony since he had already chosen on whose side he would fight.

The "collaborationist" return of the ashes was naturally to elicit the praise of those who believed in that policy. Pierre Costantini the head of the "Ligue française" proclaimed in a few leaflets that "the simple and grand gesture by Hitler was the starting point of a united Europe."

Therefore at the close of what Marcel Déat called "a kind of Florentine intrigue" the ashes of the Aiglon had returned to a country far more exposed to plunder than it had been in 1814 and 1815—to rest near the river Seine in the midst of the French people that he hadn't been given the time to love.

Outside the Dôme church to the tune of played by a French military band there were to be more cold salutes between French and German uniforms. Abetz however used the same kind of imperious attitude of the previous night.

"I expect you both immediately at the rue de Lille."

Once there they were given the sharpest kind of dressing down by the German ambassador as General Laure—who had never used that kind of language with his NCOs—was to write:

"We were subjected to a diatribe, Abetz's insane diatribe regarding what had happened the day before…He addressed himself to me, since in his mind I represented Marshal Pétain himself. As far as he was concerned I was the one responsible for what had happened. It went on for a very long time and I remained silent."

Perhaps he could have answered something…especially when Abetz hammered away:

"We remain committed to a policy of collaboration but since Italy is facing problems in the Mediterranean, the French government is showing its true face and is doing everything it can to thwart the collaboration policy. We feel it cannot be pursued with the current government. We shall take appropriate measures and shall keep it in mind when the time comes to discuss the peace treaty."

The ambassador saw his hopes go up in smoke as he was placed in a difficult position. Collaboration was necessarily tied to the policy pursued by Laval and its failure was to have a negative effect on Abetz's standing in Berlin. Should Abetz demand Laval's return or find an acceptable replacement? After all if Darlan took over and revealed himself to be a more flexible negotiator—which did in fact happen—Abetz would have managed to make the most of the situation as far as his masters in Berlin were concerned. He decided therefore to address Admiral Darlan in much less abrasive terms:

"He then turned toward Darlan and showered him with praise: the French fleet hadn't been defeated, a man of his caliber would certainly play a major role in the new and reorganized Europe."

All this was peppered with renewed attacks on certain government ministers and in particular against Peyrouton "and his cagoulards"[123] that proved how well informed Abetz was.

Darlan offered a very dignified answer:

"France is a sick and nervous country that needs to be treated carefully. Be careful not to turn it against you once again and be denied the fruits of your victory."

Laure left the two men continue alone and later as Darlan got back to his car he told Captain de Coulange who was with him:

"Do you know what is happening to me?"

Abetz is offering me the command of the European fleet the day Germany defeats England..."[124]

It was the kind of offer capable of breaking Admiral Darlan's trademark silence. Extremely vain and not too subtle did he really take Abetz's words seriously? Did he already see himself with seven stars on his sleeve like Pétain, the symbol of the most prestigious rank that had been eliminated since Murat that he often dreamed of: Admiral of France?[125]

Throughout that Sunday afternoon the crowds in Paris were allowed to pay their respects in front of the coffin of the King of Rome. The evening daily *Paris-Soir*[126] published a front page

---

123. Marcel Peyrouton was rumored to have been a member of the subversive organization "La Cagoule."

124. J. R. Tournoux, *Pétain et la France*.

125. Undoubtedly Admiral Darlan was indeed an extremely ambitious person, but it would have been very much out of character for him to confide in just any officer. Could the offer itself have jolted him out of his usual reserve? Captain de Coulange provided Jean-Raymond Tournoux, author of *Pétain et la France* (1980), with the anecdote that was also confirmed in less precise terms by General Laure. Darlan was never considered for such a promotion, in any case.

126. The version of *Paris-Soir* that the Germans authorized and where the elevator man had been promoted editor in chief since he was the only employee who had not left in the panic of June 1940.

photo of a young man laying some flowers on the tricolor draping.

It was an object of curiosity rather than of any great popular feeling. Deprived of most of their usual pastimes the Parisians didn't miss an opportunity to make a joke, by whispering:

"Instead of giving us coal they send us the remains." Or "we get a dead prisoner instead of the live ones."

That evening once the doors of the Dôme were shut the coffin was to be taken to one of side chapels within the church. But which one? Louis XIV had envisioned the Dôme church only for himself and not to receive any other dignitaries. Yet during the nineteenth century a few major figures had been placed in the six side chapels: Turenne in 1800 in the Chapel of the Virgin; Vauban in 1845 in the South Chapel; Jérôme Bonaparte, his wife and son in 1863 in the Saint Jérôme Chapel; Marshal Foch in 1937 in the Saint-Ambroise Chapel. There only remained two potential locations: the Saint-Grégoire Chapel west of the main altar (it would receive the coffin of Marshal Lyautey in 1963), decorated by Carle van Loo and the central part of the Saint-Jerôme Chapel where the tombs are located in the walls. To avoid placing the Aiglon near Marshal Foch, which could have offended the Germans, he was entombed in the central part of the Saint-Jérôme Chapel where Napoleon's coffin had been placed before the final resting place in the porphyry sarcophagus. The Aiglon was to remain in that chapel for twenty-nine years.

On December 16, the following day, the entire Parisian press corps, now working for the German occupiers, reported the event in different ways. Edouard Driault, who had worked for the return of the Aiglon nine years before and was still the President of the Institut Napoleon, made the mistake of writing on the front page of *Paris-Soir* of "a gesture that will heighten the name and the work of the Chancellor of Greater Germany."

Those words were to cause serious problems for Driault once France was liberated.

Jacques Benoist-Méchin was to write: "I sensed that those events would have serious consequences, but I didn't expect to face them so soon." The iron curtain had fallen over Franco-German relations and every advantage already secured or expected had been erased. The shadow of the Aiglon had defeated Pierre Laval but France's daily nightmare remained. Otto Abetz still believed that even though he had lost the initial battle a counter offensive could possibly allow him to regain much of the ground he had lost. On the following day he burst on the scene at Vichy with a company of SS troopers, very much the warrior and shoving aside General Laure in the elevator (the same elevator used by Marshal Pétain on his way to his daily trysts). Abetz found that Pétain was very calm and collected, definitely at his best, denying he had anything to do with Laval's arrest—in fact the Marshal had just placed a phone call lifting all surveillance at Châteldon—and even accepting to have Laval take part in the meeting. But the Marshal, who was extremely adept at providing his own defense, refused to have Laval become a government official once again. Pétain was greatly helped by the politician himself, who for once was unable to keep smiling and remain cool, as he used the raw street language of his youth as the son of an innkeeper going so far as to insult the Marshal to his face: "You're nothing but a puppet, a stuffed animal, a spinning weathercock!"

Pétain hadn't been called such names since his induction into the army. Abetz understood that things were out of hand and that he'd lost his opportunity: after all, he reasoned, it would probably be easier to bear down on Darlan than to negotiate with Laval. He returned to his formal diplomatic manner, bowed, and accepted the Marshal's invitation to lunch. After having acted Prussian Abetz went back to his urbane Rhinelander demeanor and returned to Paris much calmer in his gray green uniform with white lapels that greatly enhanced his barrel chest. He reviewed the Marshal's honor guards and saluted the flag. He did manage a small success in forcing out Colonel Groussard who joined the Resistance and getting rid of General La Laurencie whom no one attempted to defend and who was replaced by de Brinon who had been angling for the job since the beginning. When the time came to transfer the position to Brinon, La Laurencie refused to shake hands treating the new ambassador with contempt, oblivious to the fact that he was actually avoiding a situation that could have led him to a German concentration camp or a French firing squad. A few months later General La Laurencie was arrested with the labor leader Léon Jouhaux and held in custody until he regained his freedom. He embellished his role to a certain extent in his memoirs.

In the meantime at Châteldon, Pierre Laval was still being held incommunicado: he was not allowed to leave his home, the telephone lines had been cut, no one could pay him a visit nor could he write any letters.

As historian Jacques Mordal wrote: "Overseas, the coup of December 13 was very much in the news." Washington was extremely satisfied if not jubilant. Churchill made no mystery that he was very pleased by those developments. French public opinion secretly applauded Pétain's tough stand towards Hitler. At the same time the Marshal took stock of the consequences of the ousting of Laval that had been spurred by the return of the Aiglon and especially its effect on Franco-German relations.

Pétain then wrote to Adolf Hitler on December 25 in an attempt to quiet things down:

I also wish to express my sincere thanks for the noble gesture of returning a son who was denied his father's legacy by the island enemy that had defeated him.

As Henri Michel wrote:

Only one thing was certain at that time: the Marshal of France, head of the État Français in spite of his prestige and royal "We" in the manner of Louis XIV was only the little monarch of a spa, no more influential than the president of Slovakia and less free to act than the King of Bulgaria.

The end result of the return of the Aiglon's remains came on December 25 from Hitler himself, according to Darlan, who reported his words:

I was deeply outraged at the way my gesture of returning the remains of the Duke of Reichstadt to France was being interpreted.[127] The French government asked me on several occasions for my authorization to return either to Versailles or to Paris. Each time I rejected the request in the best interests of the French government so that it couldn't be said that because of its presence in Paris or Versailles it was operating under the pressure of the occupying power.

Since matters have come to what we have now I no longer wish to hear anything more about the French government returning to Paris.

I feel it is an unqualifiable infamy [bodemlose infamie] to have insinuated that I intended to draw Marshal Pétain to Paris and hold him as a prisoner. The shape of the French government and the men who are part of it are of no interest to me.[128]

---

127. On December 18 Abetz had written to Hitler: "It was said that the funeral of the Duke of Reichstadt was being held to force Pétain to name Laval as Prime Minister and limit Pétain's role to that of President of the Republic." He did not mention confining Pétain to the palace at Versailles.
128. Quoted in Alain Darlan, *L'Amiral Darlan parle*, op.cit.

Was the ruler of the German Reich telling the truth? Since he came to power he had been lying to France and historians have no reason to believe him. However were the things he was denying, true? Perhaps a plan to ambush Marshal Pétain and draw him into a trap had actually existed but since it didn't work Hitler was now in complete denial. Both versions are potentially possible. But the Nazi dictator would never forgive Pétain to have deceived him as he did.

As he left Vichy defeated by the Aiglon's ghost, Pierre Laval had said:

"I will no longer look for friends among the French and will find them among the Germans."[129] Laval returned to Paris in the same railroad car as Abetz and as subdued as King Frederic William III after the battle of Jena. Laval then wrote the following rather incredible letter to Hitler:

Mister Reich Chancellor,

I wish to express my sincere thanks through this letter.
I have been the victim of a ridiculous aggression by the police. I was able to hear on the radio with the deepest joy during the house arrest I had been assigned to, the statement by the Ambassador to the newspapers.

The next day I found out that your Ambassador was going to Vichy and that he would then pay me a visit at Châteldon. I concluded that I would soon be free and that I owed this to you.

The policy of collaboration with Germany has met with the approval of a majority of Frenchmen. The numbers of those who understand that it is the only direction we can go are growing by the day.

I love my country and I know it can find a worthy place in the New Europe that you are building.

---

129. Ibid.

Due to the position you have taken, Mister Reich Chancellor, I feel entitled to believe that you agree with the sincerity of my efforts. You have not been mistaken that I had misinterpreted the magnanimous grandeur that you had shown by offering the path of collaboration to France immediately following your victory.

Mister Reich Chancellor kindly accept the assurance of my highest regard and of my faithful salutation.

Pierre Laval[130]

It was clearly an expression of gratitude and an offer of services: "A monstrous letter," according to a German historian; "A letter of treason," wrote Robert Aron. As J.P. Cointet wrote:

"An attitude grossly overestimating his own image and charisma."

In any case it was the worthy conclusion of six months of political indecency. Napoleon had shown greater dignity at Saint Helena even though he was being held as a prisoner by a foreign enemy. Laval had only been a prisoner of the French.

As Victor Vinde wrote in 1942:

Whoever met Pierre Laval at the end of 1940 could clearly see that he no longer was the self-assured triumphant man who at Vichy was shaping his country in new ways. He was by then a prophet who had become disenchanted with his fellow citizens, full of bitterness and rather exhausted. He had to accept the fact that the masses that he despised so much were necessary for the support of the regime and give it strength—but the masses hated Pierre Laval—I am the most unpopular man in France, he used to say with a wry smile. That was a conclusion that history certainly did confirm.

---

130. This letter was published by Otto Abetz.

For a brief moment a few days later it was possible to think that Napoleon's victorious aura had once again returned to the French army. On January 17 the French navy in Indochina had completely destroyed the Thaï naval forces that had attacked it: it would be the only French naval victory of the entire war that can be attributed to the Vichy government. In any case Vichy had managed to recapture some of its prestige overseas. Churchill wrote a personal letter to Pétain at the end of 1940 while the *Times* mentioned "the daring and energetic decisions of Marshal Pétain" and "the honor of that dignified and solitary figure." These were the Marshal's One Hundred days that were to last much longer but in a continuous and unstoppable decline.[131]

Then silence once again reigned supreme under the Dôme of the Invalides. Pierre Laval was able to convince himself that he had always been right and was returned to power in April 1942.[132] He pursued the same policy and eliminated those who took part in the conspiracy especially du Moulin de la Barthète who was named commercial attaché in Switzerland where he was able to trace his own steps.[133] It was only once he reached

---

131. Abetz, who by then was much less of a Francophile, was recalled to Germany in November 1942 and sent back to Paris in December 1943 with new instructions calling for extreme firmness. He was arrested by French forces in October 1945 and condemned to twenty years' hard labor in 1949. Abetz was pardoned in 1954 he died in an automobile accident in 1958. He managed to write his memoirs while in prison at Fresnes and the Cherche-midi, *Histoire d'une politique franco-allemande,* 1953.

132. Laval's return to power prompted the resignation of Marcel Peyrouton whom Darlan had sent to Argentina the year before. After the allied landings in North Africa, Peyrouton offered to serve Darlan and Giraud who appointed him governor general of Algeria (January to June 1943). When de Gaulle arrived in Algiers Peyrouton went to Morocco to take command of a military unit but was placed under house arrest in November 1943 and spent several years in semi-captivity. He was acquitted in 1948 and wrote his memoirs, *Du service public à la prison commune* (1950). He died in 1983 at the age of 96.

133. The reporter Claude Salvy was to write in 1946: "We answered your systematic denunciations by not listening to them. It was natural for the country to emerge divided. Had I been on your side I would have also been

Sigmaringen after he had left France and witnessed Germany's total defeat that Laval said: "How could I have made such a mistake?"

This history of official burials was to have one more adventurous episode at the end of the war. As the German occupation wore on the French public forgot all about the Aiglon and became more and more preoccupied with its daily problems and hopes for the future. At the beginning of 1944 two German officers appeared at the office of an attorney André Dussol who represented the city of Paris but was also the grand provost of the "Blue Penitents" a religious brotherhood that handled burials in several provincial cities. The chapel of the Blue Penitents located in the rue des Etudes was the burial location of Albine de Montholon, a friend and possibly also the lover of Napoleon at Saint-Helena. Her mummified body dressed in a gown was kept as it is today inside a glass coffin in the chapel.

Those polite and very well informed German officers came to request that the Grand Provost agree to ship the body of Albine to the Invalides. Attorney Dussol and the local authorities did their best to avoid the transfer since the German occupiers were no longer in a position to enforce their demands. D-Day and the invasion of France by the Allies interrupted any such requests as the Germans focused on the fighting. However Dussol was able to describe this odd request in 1996.[134]

What was the meaning of that strange story? After returning Napoleon's son to his father did Hitler also seek to reunite the

---

uncompromising about Marshal Pétain as a mere transition. Since I lived through it in intense anxiety for two years, I must say that it was not at all what you think. Yes there was weakness, the inability to take action, the focus on regenerating France instead of resisting, the heavy and useless burdens, and the too many offensive measures imposed on the French people. But no, there certainly never was willful treason."

134. See Alain Decaux, *Morts pour Vichy*, Paris 2000. See G. Poisson, *L'Aventure du retour des cendres* Paris 2004.

Emperor with his last mistress? When the dictator committed suicide the following year with Eva Braun was he still thinking about that odd companion of Napoleon's defeat?[135]

Pétain and Laval were both forced to leave Vichy under German escort in July 1944. They left a devastated France, bombed by the Allies, tens of thousands of victims deported to concentration camps, the dishonor of having handed over countless thousands to the Nazis, the shame of Frenchmen wearing a German uniform, the French army and navy wiped out and in exchange the coffin of the Aiglon that no one can see to this day...[136]

---

135. See Dussol's story in René Maury, *Albine, le dernier amour de Napoléon* Paris 1998.
136. See Jacques Macé, *L'honneur retrouvé du général de Montholon*, Paris 2000. If that bizarre project had come to fruition where would the remains of the poor Albine been placed inside the Dôme? Perhaps in a small location invisible to the public like King Louis-Philippe had arranged for his mother's friend Rouzet at Dreux.

8.

Epilog:
The Fate of a Tomb

Following the ceremony of December 15, 1940 and the many visits of curious Parisians, the Invalides administration had to get down to business. To begin with there were money matters and it was naturally the French treasury that was called upon to foot the bill for a ceremony the Germans had imposed. A budget of 150,000 francs was deemed necessary requiring an authorization for expenditures signed by "the Marshal of France, head of the French State." It was an old habit of the Third Republic to have top officials sign off on the smallest administrative spending. Among the payments were the bills of the Borniol funeral services that included flags, rugs, chairs, candlesticks and even a gurney: that total came to 27,128 francs.

Even though it turned out to be a failure, some ultra collaborationists were determined to keep the spirit of the event alive. The "Youth for the New Europe" of the *Collaboration* group decided to organize a funeral wake in December 1942 around the Aiglon's coffin. Brinon was present and gave the Nazi salute.[137] Abetz and Taittinger were also there along with young members of Déat's movement in black shirts with red armbands. They repeated the ceremony in January 1943 and caused some damage when photographers climbed on top of the monument to King Jérôme to be able to photograph the event from a high angle. The same group was to organize a final wake in June 1944 perhaps in the hope that the Aiglon would rise up against the Allies that had just landed in Normandy. The only result was to create more damage and some 19,544 francs in administrative costs.

At the same time a permanent location for the coffin was being discussed. Robert de Beauplan had suggested in 1940 that the Aiglon be placed at the foot of Napoleon's tomb that would have been a poor arrangement. Others on the contrary, wanted to enclose the coffin in a monumental tomb like the other tombs in the Dôme church. There was however no space in the center of the Saint-Jérôme chapel for such a monument and it would have also duplicated the mistake made with Joseph Bonaparte's tomb that proved to be too large for the Saint Augustine chapel. Keeping the Aiglon in the Chapel of Saint-Jérôme with or without a monumental tomb would have set Napoleon's son among a number of unrelated tombs from various historical periods (marshals of Louis XIV, Napoleonic family members, marshals of the Republic). A man who had legitimately been Emperor of the French for a total of two weeks deserved a second rank placement just behind his father. Furthermore by moving the coffin the authorities could also erase any memory of Hitler's involvement.

Inside the crypt, just opposite the entrance there is a small square room of about twelve square meters that is often called

---

137. Fernand de Brinon was tried and shot for treason on April 15, 1947.

the "cella." In 1846 Visconti had managed to place a statue of the Emperor Napoleon by Simurd that is still standing at that location. In the center of this "Chapel of relics" there is a window display with the sword of Austerlitz, Napoleon's hat from the battle of Eylau, a grand Cordon of the Legion of Honor and the keys to the ebony coffin. The tomb of the Aiglon could easily replace the window display at the foot of the statue, a plan of this kind was drafted in April 1941.

The issue took twenty-eight years to be resolved and architect Jean-Pierre Paquet had enough time to supervise the entire operation. The long period from the Occupation to the Fifth Republic was marked by innumerable procrastination of one kind or another. Should the coffin remain where it had been placed in 1940 (in the chapel of Saint-Jérôme) or should it be moved to the cella? Should it be on view or part of a monumental tomb? Would it replace the Emperor's statue or not? There were visits, meetings among commissions and committees to discuss the matter, each one separated by periods of silence and expectation while the issue remained always tainted by the memory of Hitler's part in the affair. Each solution had its supporters until finally in February 1969 just before leaving office General de Gaulle approved the change without giving it much thought.

But how would the operation be handled? In order to build a monumental tomb the Emperor's statue had to be removed but there was some hesitation to making any "correction." Visconti and the high commission for Historical Monuments ruled against it.[138] Was the answer then to place the coffin at the foot of the statue? This could be done but the two pieces of sculpture would not blend in easily and father and son would be "fighting"

---

138. Since this architectural ensemble was in the basement, the recess holding the statue of Napoleon could be set further in gaining needed space. It would also solve the issue of the statue's scepter since it was too long for the recess. But the commission members don't always study the issues on the spot.

for attention.[139] The idea of building a monumental tomb was dropped and a different and regrettable solution was chosen instead. The bronze casket was termed to be "of no interest" and it was then buried deep inside the chapel[140] marking it simply with a bronze plaque with an inscription, coat of arms and emblems. The final result was the opposite of the original intent of showing the casket within a monumental tomb. It was now completely invisible.[141]

Even that solution was found to be too complicated and difficult to carry out. Once the window display and the relics were removed a grave was excavated where the bronze sarcophagus with all its moldings was placed. It was now completely invisible where during the Habsbourg period it had been on view for over a century in the crypt of the Capuchins. The bronze plaque and the ornaments were also dispensed with and the following inscription was written on the floor:

Napoleon II

Roi de Rome

1811–1832

The operation took place on December 10, 1969, the day of the solemn transfer with Republican Guards, a Handel concerto, the royal march by Gossec in the presence of Prince and Princess Napoleon.

For a long time it was thought that the Aiglon would have a spectacular location within the Dôme church, but in the end his

---

139. Without touching the statue the space available in the chapel was 3.97 meters by 3.14 meters, while the sarcophagus measured 2.55 by 0.70 wide.

140. We should recall that a similar solution was used some years ago for the caskets of the kings at Saint-Denis where the locations are marked by large marble slabs. The author is responsible for the names of the kings being inscribed on each of the slabs.

141. Even a photograph of the coffin cannot be found at commercial photo agencies.

memory was erased almost completely. Grief had followed him throughout his life and even beyond, into death. Everything he had attempted ended in failure: his short life denied him his throne and ended in exile, he died far from his homeland under a different name, his return to France came at the whim of the occupying enemy, even his tomb was all but forgotten by an indifferent public.

Along with the celebration of the two hundredth anniversary of the French Empire, in 2011 we shall celebrate the anniversary of the birth of the heir to the imperial throne and for the occasion some improvements are being made.[142] May we hope to see once more the beautiful casket of Napoleon's son?

---

142. The Army Museum (Musée de l'Armée) is currently working on building two tunnels that will surround the crypt: one commemorating the exile, death, and return of the Emperor and the other dedicated to Napoleon II.

Cast of Characters

OTTO ABETZ (1903–1958)

Trained as an art teacher, Otto Abtez had a job at a girl's school in Karlsruhe. Active in the Nazi Party since 1931, he became a liaison between German and French war veterans' associations. Joined the SS and the Foreign Ministry in 1935, he married a French woman Suzanne de Bruyker who had been the secretary of newspaper editor Jean Luchaire (see below). Abetz was a founder of the Comité France-Allemagne and an ardent Francophile. In 1938 Abtez was present at the Munich conference and represented certain Nazi interests in Paris in 1938-39 until he was expelled on suspicion of espionage. Upon returning to France in June 1940, he was assigned to the Paris embassy where at first he was in charge of seizing art collections particularly those belonging to French Jews. The confiscated art was stored at the Louvre museum. In August 1940 Abetz was appointed ambassador to the French government at Vichy, but continued to reside in Paris. While traditional German diplomats disliked Abetz as a Nazi careerist, he gained the trust of Joachim von Ribbentrop and firmly believed and promoted the policy of collaboration by supporting Pierre Laval. The German embassy also became a meeting ground for the art world in occupied Paris and Abetz entertained lavishly. He demanded the deportation of foreign Jews early on in 1940–41; his influence was greatly diminished after the occupation of the free zone (zone libre) on November 11, 1942. Even though he fell in disfavor with Hitler and von Ribbentrop he remained as ambassador until September 1944. Captured in 1945, he was sentenced to 20 years of hard labor in 1949 by a French court for war crimes, in particular for his role in sending French Jews to the death camps. Released in 1954, he died in an automobile accident in 1958 on the Cologne autobahn. He left a book of memoirs: *Histoire d'une politique franco-allemande* (Paris, 1953).

ERNST ACHENBACH (1909–1991)

Ernst Achenbach was a lawyer and diplomat who studied law in Paris and Berlin and joined the German foreign ministry in 1936. In 1940–1943 Achenbach headed the political section of the Paris embassy, working closely with Abetz where he was known to be anti-French. In 1946 he was practicing law in Essen, was active in politics in Westpahlia, and in European Union matters; he continued to practice law until 1976.

RAPHAËL ALIBERT (1887–1963)

An eminent jurist and law professor at the École des Sciences Politiques since 1923, he was known for his extreme conservative views. Under secretary of state to the prime minister in June–July 1940, Alibert was appointed minister of justice by Marshal Pétain from July to December 1940. He ordered the arrest of Marcel Déat on December 14, 1940, then was demoted to Undersecretary of Justice until January 1941 and dismissed because of his vocal anti-German views. Condemned by a French court in March 1947, Alibert was responsible for the enactment of the early anti-Semitic laws and regulations in particular the "Statut des Juifs" in October 1940. Pétain said later that Alibert gave him flawed advice and thought he was mentally deranged.

PAUL BAUDOIN (1894–1964)

A graduate of the prestigious École Polytechnique Paul Baudoin became a director of the Banque de l'Indochine and was considered a technocrat. In March 1940 he was appointed by his friend Paul Reynaud as under secretary of state; he became Foreign Minister in the Pétain government from June 1940 to October 28, 1940 when Laval replaced him. Rather than face demotion, Baudoin resigned from all government posts a few weeks later.

BARON JACQUES BENOIST-MÉCHIN (1901–1983)

Historian, talented journalist, and translator, Benoist-Méchin worked at various newspapers and magazines and became chief editor at *L'Intransiegeant* in 1930. He joined the fascist Parti Populaire Français (PPF) led by Jacques Doriot in 1936. Author of a multi volume *Histoire de l'armée allemande* (History of the German Army) published in 1938 which Colonel de Gaulle read and admired at the time. In close contact with Otto Abetz as early as 1938 he repeatedly visited Berlin before the war on veterans matters. In 1941–1942 was appointed under secretary of state for foreign affairs by Admiral Darlan, he joined the LVF (Legion of French Volunteers in Russia). Captured and tried he was condemned to death in 1947 but was quickly reprieved and saw his sentence commuted, until he was freed in 1954. While in prison he developed an interest in Islam and he later wrote many books and articles on the Middle East and North Africa as well as two volumes of memoirs.

LOUIS-NAPOLÉON BONAPARTE (1808–1873)

Prince Louis-Napoléon Bonaparte, as he was known before becoming emperor as Napoleon III, was born in Paris. He was the third son of Hortense de Beauharnais, the daughter of Josephine de Beauharnais by her first marriage, and of Louis Bonaparte, a younger brother of Napoléon I, making him the emperor's nephew. His parents had been made king and queen of Holland. After being elected president of the Second Republic Louis-Napoleon staged a coup d'état in Paris in 1851 and proclaimed the Second Empire. His reign ended with France's defeat by Prussia in the war of 1870.

YVES BOUTHILLER (1901–1977)

Head of the cabinet of the Finance Ministry in 1931–1939, he became Finance Minister in June 1940, and was closely involved in Laval's dismissal and arrest in December 1940. He remained Minister of National Economy until Laval's return in 1942. He went on trial in 1947 and was later declared innocent. He joined the Banque Nationale de Paris and was elected mayor of Saint-Martin-de-Ré a post to which he was reelected for many years.

MARQUIS FERNAND DE BRINON (1885–1947)

Journalist and politician he studied law and developed an interest in improving Franco-German relations as early as 1920. He created the Comité France-Allemagne with Otto Abetz, he obtained a sensational interview with Adolf Hitler in 1933 and wrote many articles favorable to Nazi Germany. In 1940 he worked directly for Pierre Laval in Paris and was appointed as Vichy's representative to the German authorities with the rank of ambassador and secretary of state. In August-September 1944 he followed the German retreat to Sigmaringen castle, where he was put in charge of a rump pro-Nazi French government in exile. Tried for treason and condemned to death, he was executed by firing squad in 1947.

COUNT RENÉ DE CHAMBRUN (1906–2002)

Chambrun married Pierre Laval's daughter Josée in 1935. An international lawyer and at one point head of the Baccarat crystal works, Chambrun was a direct descendant of the Marquis de Lafayette. He was awarded dual American and French citizenship by Franklin D. Roosevelt in 1940 and served as a go-between for Prime Minister Paul Reynaud during the fall of France. Chambrun was a staunch defender of Pierre Laval's memory and appeared in the film, *The Sorrow and the Pity*. With his wife Chambrun also created a foundation to publish and study the papers and works of Lafayette.

JEAN-FRANÇOIS DARLAN (1881–1942)

A graduate of the École Navale, Darlan served in the French Navy in the Far East and was appointed head of the cabinet at the Ministry of Marine then Navy chief of staff in 1937. Promoted Admiral of the Fleet in 1939, he became Minister of Marine in the Pétain government on June 16, 1940. Anti-British, he opted for a collaborationist policy and replaced Laval after his arrest as Deputy Prime Minister. He met with Hitler on December 25, 1940, and was named Pétain's official successor. Darlan agreed to allow German aircraft to use French bases in Syria but the plan was criticized by General Weygand and immediately withdrawn. In April 1942 he was replaced by Pierre Laval. In November 1942 in Algiers, he signed an agreement with General Mark Clark ending the allegiance of French North Africa to Vichy. He was assassinated in Algiers on December 24,

1942, by Bonnier de la Chapelle, a young Gaullist assisted by British SOE agents.

PIERRE COSTANTINI (1889–1986)

Costantini was originally from Corsica, and frequently used the alias of Pierre Dominique. he was A passionate admirer of Napoleon he was wounded in the First World War. A militant right-wing journalist he joined the extremist Cagoule terrorist group. He was rabidly anti-British and published a book about Napoleon with German censorship approval in 1940. In 1941 he founded the Ligue Française, a splinter anti-Semitic and pro-Nazi party allied to the PPF of Jacques Doriot. In 1944 Costantini was able to avoid prison by being declared mentally incompetent and spent ten years in a psychiatric hospital. During the 1960s using his pen name of Pierre Dominique, Costantini wrote articles in right-wing publications such as *Ecrits de Paris* and *Rivarol*.

MARCEL DÉAT (1894–1955)

A graduate of the École Normale Supérieure and "agrégé" in philosophy, Déat started out in politics in 1926 as a socialist deputy to parliament. He was reelected in 1932 and promptly excluded from the official socialist party (SFIO) in 1933 because of his anti-Marxist views. In 1935 he was very briefly Minister of the Air Force and in 1936 was defeated in the elections that saw the victory of the Popular Front. He returned to parliament in 1939 and was a pacifist and a harsh critic of the war. He vigorously promoted a single party fascist-type political system which Laval and Pétain rejected. In 1940 he became the founder of a daily collaborationist newspaper, *L'Œuvre,* where he constantly attacked Vichy as being too soft and traditional. He was arrested in Paris on December 14, 1940, and released a few hours later by the German embassy. A virulent anti-Semite, Déat was the most extreme in demanding that France be totally aligned on Nazi Germany and would have certainly preferred a Quisling-type government to Vichy. He finally became a minister in the last Vichy government in 1944 and then fled to Germany after the liberation of Paris. He spent the rest of his life in hiding in a convent in Italy where wrote his memoirs.

JACQUES DORIOT (1898–1945)

Communist leader and deputy in 1924, known for his violent agitation against the colonial war in the Rif (Morocco) in 1925, and his anti-militarist propaganda speeches, Doriot was elected mayor of Saint Denis, a working class suburb of Paris. He was ousted from the Communist Party in June 1934 after an ideological disagreement. Doriot immediately took positions radically opposed to the communists and founded the PPF (Parti Populaire Français) that was violently anti-Semitic and modeled on Fascism and Nazism. Critical of Vichy for being far too soft, Doriot was one of the founders of the LVF (Légion des Volontaires Français) against bolshevism and he personally fought on the Russian front in a German uniform in 1941–42. He was killed in Germany in February 1945 when his car was machine gunned by an Allied fighter plane.

EDOUARD DRUMONT (1844–1917)

Journalist and writer Drumont published a two-volume pamphlet, *La France Juive,* in 1886 that was a violently anti-Semitic attack on foreign Jews living in France. In 1892 he founded a daily newspaper, *La Libre Parole,* that also took an extreme anti-Semitic line. He relentlessly attacked Capt. Alfred Dreyfus accusing him unjustly of being a traitor and as an Alsatian Jew a German agent. Drumont was to influence many right-wing

French writers and politicians including Charles Maurras and Léon Daudet as well as the Action Française in general. His two volume anti-Semitic pamphlet was reprinted in 1941 by Flammarion in Paris with German support.

PIERRE-ÉTIENNE FLANDIN (1889–1958)

Politician and cabinet minister during the 1930s, and prime minister from November 1934 to May 1935 when Pierre Laval was his foreign minister, Flandin promoted the Stresa conference with Mussolini and the British government. A convinced pacifist he applauded the Munich agreements of September 1938 and sent a telegram congratulating Hitler on his success. At Vichy, he wanted to replace Pierre Laval in 1940 and was appointed foreign minister on December 13, by Marshal Pétain but his appointment as deputy prime minister was rejected by the German authorities. Flandin quickly left Vichy in February 1941 and was replaced by Admiral Darlan. Flandin was later condemned by the High Court of justice to five years of "national indignity" but was pardoned because of the help he gave to the resistance.

GENERAL CHARLES DE GAULLE (1890–1970)

Born in Lille, son of a professor of classics at the Catholic Institute De Gaulle attended the Collège Stanislas where he prepared his entry examination to St. Cyr Military Academy and graduated as a lieutenant in 1913. He attended the lectures of Colonel Pétain at the École de guerre and served in the First World War until he was captured. Promoted to major in 1920, he was a lecturer at St. Cyr in 1921 and at the École de guerre in 1922; he became part of Marshal Pétain's cabinet in 1925 when the marshal was vice president of the Supreme War Council. As a colonel in 1940, De Gaulle commanded a motorized unit and fought in the Ardennes. Promoted to brigadier general, he was appointed under secretary of war by Paul Reynaud in June 1940. He left Bordeaux for London with General Edward Spears on June 16, 1940, and created the Free French movement with his first broadcast speech on BBC radio on June 18, 1940. De Gaulle rejected the armistice and called on all Frenchmen to join him and fight the Germans. In 1943 he became head of the Provisional Government in Algiers and then in Paris in 1944. Opposed to the constitution of the Fourth Republic, De Gaulle resigned in 1946 and created a political party, the RPF, also known as the "Gaullist party." When he returned to power in May 1958, he founded the Fifth Republic and remained president until his resignation in 1969. General de Gaulle is the author among other books, of three volumes of war memoirs published in the 1950s.

ÉDOUARD HERRIOT (1872–1957)

Son of an army officer and trained as a teacher Herriot went into politics and became mayor of Lyon in 1905 as a member of the center left Radical Socialist party. He was often a government minister and served as prime minister three times. Herriot's career in government began in 1916 and ended in 1954. He was also elected to the French Academy in 1946. From 1936 to 1940, he was president of the Chamber of Deputies until the vote of July 10, 1940, giving full powers to Marshal Pétain. At odds with Vichy he was placed on trial at the court in Riom, then arrested and imprisoned by the Gestapo when the Nazis suspected that he was about to escape to the United States. Franklin D. Roosevelt knew and liked Herriot best among all French politicians and thought of placing him at the head of a French government in exile. Herriot was known as one of the great orators of the French parliament as well as a prolific writer.

GENERAL BENOÎT FORNEL DE LA LAURENCIE (1879–1958)

He distinguished himself as commander of the Third Army Corps in 1940 at Dunkirk. In August 1940 Marshal Pétain appointed him as representative of the Vichy government to the German military authorities in Paris. He was involved in the arrest of Marcel Déat on December 14, 1940, and dismissed on German insistence. He was replaced by the pro-Nazi Fernand de Brinon. Later at Vichy La Laurencie was dismissed a second time for making anti-German statements.

GENERAL AUGUSTE LAURE (1881–1957)

Commander of the French IX Corps 1939–1940, commander, French 8th Army 1940; General Laure was taken prisoner by the Germans 1940. He was released on Pétain's personal request and appointed military secretary to Marshal Pétain in 1940–1942. He was arrested by the Gestapo and sent to Germany 1943–1945. Laure was acquitted on charges of collaboration because of services rendered to the French resistance. General de Gaulle eulogized Laure at his death.

PIERRE LAVAL (1883–1945)

From humble beginnings at Châteldon, in central France, Laval became a lawyer in Paris in 1907 and joined the Socialist Party. He was elected mayor of the working class suburb of Aubervilliers in 1924 and deputy to parliament. He quickly veered to the right abandoning socialism. He became Prime Minister in 1931 and again in 1935 until January 1936. He opposed the Popular Front and supported the Munich agreements in 1938. In June 1940 he created the Vichy regime and became Deputy Prime Minister in the government of Marshal Pétain. Ousted by the monarchists and technocrats at Vichy on

December 13, 1940, he was freed by Otto Abetz and returned to power in April 1942 to enact a policy of total collaboration. The harsh measures against the Jews and the major deportations took place under his administration which progressively resembled a Quisling government bowing to German demands. Laval however remained a creature of the parliamentary system and in August 1944 he even attempted to hand over power to Edouard Herriot. Laval was taken to Germany then captured and returned to France to stand trial for treason. Found guilty, he was shot by a firing squad in 1945.

ALBERT LEBRUN (1871–1950)

A graduate of the École Polytechnique Lebrun was elected president of the Republic in 1932 and reelected in 1939. In 1940 he remained passive in the face of defeat and his only active protest was to try and save Georges Mandel when he was arrested by the Germans. After the Vichy vote of July 10, 1940, Lebrun retired from politics and was eventually arrested by the Germans in 1943 but quickly freed. He retired from politics after the war.

JEAN LUCHAIRE (1901–1946)

Journalist at *Le Petit Parisien,* Luchaire created a monthly magazine, *Notre Temps,* in 1927, supported by the French foreign ministry and Aristide Briand. He met Otto Abetz in 1932 and organized Franco-German meetings and exchanges. A right-wing pacifist he was in favor of Munich and in 1940 used his friendship with Abetz and Laval to his own benefit as a fervent promoter of Franco-German collaboration. He created a new daily, *Les Nouveaux Temps,* in November 1940 and became the head of the all powerful Paris press association. He called for ultracollaboration all the way to the end in 1944 and fled to

Germany with Brinon. Luchaire was condemned for treason and executed by firing squad in February 1946.

GEORGES MANDEL (1885–1944)

Born Louis Rothschild he was the son of a tailor, his family was not related to the banking dynasty and was Jewish. He became a journalist at *L'Aurore* a daily newspaper owned by Clemenceau who later hired Mandel as his personal assistant during the First World War. Elected to parliament in 1919, he served many times as a government minister especially as minister of the Colonies in 1938–1940. He was Minister of the Interior in the last Reynaud government in 1940. Mandel refused to fly to London with de Gaulle and General Spears choosing to go to Morocco with 25 other deputies instead. Unable to contact Churchill in an attempt to form a government in exile in North Africa he was arrested in Casablanca by General Noguès acting on orders from Laval, and forcibly returned to France where he was imprisoned with other anti-Vichy French politicians. In 1944 the Gestapo handed Mandel over to the extremist pro-Nazi "Milice française" in retaliation for the assassination of Philippe Henriot, the collaborationist minister of propaganda. Two months later Mandel was executed at Fontainebleau in July 1944.

CHARLES MAURRAS (1868–1952)

A poet and writer Maurras is best known as a political journalist and polemicist, he was elected to the Académie Française in 1939. He came to politics during the Dreyfus Affair in 1899 when the Action Française movement was created by Maurice Pujo and Henri Vaugeois. A newspaper called *L'Action Française* was also launched to support the doctrine calling for "integral nationalism" elaborated by Maurras. The ideology was based on the superiority of French culture and extreme forms of xenophobia: Jews, half-breeds and Freemasons were to be suppressed and deported but not necessarily killed. Maurras remained an extreme anti-German to the end and moved his newspaper to Lyon in the unoccupied zone in 1940 to avoid strict German control. At the height of its popularity in the 1920s, Action Française had over 100,000 members and readers. Its influence was greatly reduced by the condemnation by the Vatican in 1926 on theological grounds excommunicating Maurras and the rise of French Fascism in the 1930s. French Fascists were nationalists and learned from Maurras before moving on to more extreme parties. The first period of Vichy in 1940 was definitely inspired by the "Maurassien" ideology and dominated by traditional monarchists. But even Marshal Pétain, although he agreed with many of Maurras' ideas, kept his distance. Maurras was tried and condemned for treason but released due to ill health in 1952; he died a few months later.

DR. BERNARD MÉNÉTREL (1906–1947)

The personal physician of Marshal Pétain was the son of a military doctor. He played an important and secret political role at Vichy and was always seen with the Marshal. Rumors circulated that he was actually Pétain's illegitimate son. He always opposed Laval and in 1944 he was arrested by the Gestapo, freed, and then rearrested by French forces in 1945. In 1946 he was freed from prison and died in an automobile accident a year later without ever seeing his only patient, Marshal Pétain, again.

HENRI DU MOULIN DE LABARTHÈTE (1900–1948)

Lawyer and army officer du Moulin served in Syria in 1921–23 and then joined the finance ministry. From 1931 to 1934 was the director of the cabinet of Paul Reynaud then minister of the colonies. From July 1940 to April 1942, he headed Marshal

Pétain's civilian cabinet. From August 1942 to 1945 he was financial attaché at the French embassy in Bern.

MARCEL PEYROUTON (1887–1983)

Son-in-law of a deputy to parliament, the controversial Louis Malvy, Peyrouton was a Freemason, a lawyer and an energetic colonial administrator. He joined the ministry of the colonies in 1910. Resident general (governor) in Tunisia in 1933–1936, in 1936 Peyrouton was appointed resident general in Morocco but was immediately forced to resign by the new Prime Minster Léon Blum after the Popular Front won the elections in June. After serving as ambassador to Argentina 1936–1940, he returned to Tunisia as resident general for one month in June–July 1940. He was then appointed minister of the interior at Vichy in 1940 and was the main mover in the ouster and arrest of Pierre Laval. He returned as ambassador to Argentina in 1942 until he was appointed Governor General of Algeria from January to June 1943. He was arrested in 1944 and then pardoned in 1949 when he retired from public life.

PAUL REYNAUD (1878–1966)

Lawyer and conservative politician elected to parliament in 1928, justice minister in 1932, and later minister of the colonies, Reynaud opposed the Popular Front and supported the military theories of Colonel de Gaulle. Minster of Justice then Finance Minister in 1938–1940, Reynaud was prime minister from March to June 1940 and unsuccessfully attempted to stem the German onslaught that overran France. Arrested and taken to Germany, he was at risk of being executed by the Milice in 1944. Reelected to parliament after the war, he was a minister in several governments including deputy prime minister until 1954.

XAVIER VALLAT (1891–1972)

Vallat was a lawyer and officer in WWI and was elected to parliament in 1919. Inspired by the monarchist right-wing Action Française, Vallat was a vocal anti-Semite, an anti-Freemason with strong anti-Protestant views. Marshal Pétain appointed him to manage the veterans associations into a "Légion des combattants" but the Germans were wary of the ultra-nationalist Vallat and Abetz demanded his removal on December 17, 1940. Admiral Darlan later appointed him to be the first High Commissioner for Jewish Affairs in 1941. Vallat was much too anti-German and had to be removed in 1942 and replaced by the infamous Darquier de Pellepoix. In 1947 he was condemned to ten years in prison but was soon pardoned and resumed his old anti-Semitic propaganda as editor of the weekly newspaper *Aspects de la France*—heir to Maurras' Action Française—from 1962 to 1966.

GENERAL MAXIME WEYGAND (1867–1965)

Born in Belgium and thought to be the illegitimate son of King Leopold II of Belgium, Weygand graduated from St. Cyr in 1887. An outspoken anti-Dreyfus officer he was also vocally anti-Semitic. On the staff of Marshal Foch he became a brilliant strategist in the First World War. He read out the armistice conditions to the Germans in November 1918 in the railroad car at Compiègne. He was sent to Warsaw in 1920 to help Poland against the Soviets. A legend surrounding his brilliant military leadership in Poland has been recently debunked. In 1931 was appointed High Commissioner in Syria and retired in 1935. He returned to Syria in 1939 and on May 19, 1940, became Commander in Chief of the French army replacing General Maurice Gamelin as the battle raged across northern France. He was in favor of the armistice and remained in the Vichy government as Minister of Defense until the Germans demanded that he be removed. He was then sent to North Africa where he rebuilt the French army in the expectation of getting back into the war on the Allied side. Weygand had close contacts with American diplomat Robert Murphy who tried unsuccessfully to have Wyegand repudiate Vichy and come over to the Allies. He was arrested at Vichy by the Gestapo and taken to Germany. Arrested briefly in Paris in 1946, Weygand was cleared of collaborationism in 1948 and lived until he was 98.

Bibliography

Abetz, Otto, *Pétain et les Allemands*, Gaucher, 1948.

Alméras, Philippe, *Un Français nommé Pétain*, Paris, R. Laffont, 1995.

Amouroux, Henri, *Pour en finir avec Vichy*, t. 2: *Les racines des passions*, 1940–1941, Paris, R. Laffont, 2005.

Aron, Robert, *Histoire de Vichy*, Paris, A. Sauret, 1954.

Aubry, Octave, *L'Aiglon, des Tuileries aux Invalides*, Paris 1941.

Azéma, J. P., *La Collaboration*, Paris, Presses universitaires de France, 1975.

Azéma, J. P., F. Bédarida, *La France des années noires*, Paris Éditions du Seuil, 2000.

Azéma, J. P., O. Wievorka, *Vichy 1940–1944*, Paris, Perrin, 2000.

Baudoin, Paul, *Neuf mois au gouvernement*, Paris, Éditions de la Table Ronde, 1948.

Benjamin, René, *Le Grand Homme seul*, Paris, Plon, 1943.

Benoist-Méchin, Jacques, *De la défaite au désastre*, t. I, Paris Albin Michel, 1985.

——, *À l'épreuve du temps*, Paris, Julliard, 1989.

Bourget, Pierre, *Un certain Philippe Pétain*, Paris, Casterman, 1966.

Bouthillier, Yves, *Le Drame de Vichy*, Paris, Plon, 1950.

Brinon, Fernand de, *À ses amis*, s.l., S.I., 1947 *Mémoires*, Paris, L.L.C., 1949.

Burrin, Philippe, *La France à l'heure allemande, 1940–1944*, Paris, Éditions du Seuil, 1994.

Cars, Jean des, *Rodolphe et les secrets de Mayerling*, Paris, Perrin, 2004.

Chambrun, René de, *Pierre Laval devant l'Histoire*, Paris, France-Empire, 1983.

——, *Le Château de Schoenbrunn*, Vienne, 1986.

Choffat, Thierry, *Le retour des cendres de l'Aiglon en 1940. Un coup d'État bonapartiste?*, Centre d'Études et de Recherches sur le Bonapartisme, été 2006.

Cointet, Michèle et Jean-Paul, *Dictionnaire historique de la France sous l'Occupation*, Paris, Tallandier, 2000.

Cointet, Michèle, *Vichy capitale 1940–1944*, Paris, Perrin, 1993.

Cointet, Jean-Paul, *Pierre Laval*, Paris, Fayard, 1993; *Histoire de Vichy*, Paris, Perrin, 2003.

Cole, Hubert, *Pierre Laval*, Paris, Fayard, 1964.

Cotta, Michèle, *La Collaboration*, Paris, A. Colin, 1964.

Coutau-Bégarie, Hervé et Huan, Claude, *Darlan*, Paris, Fayard, 1989.

Darlan, Alain, *L'Admiral Darlan parle*, Paris, Amiot-Dumont, 1953.

Déat, Marcel, *Mémoires politiques*, Paris, Denoël, 1989

Deck, René, *Le Retour des cendres du Roi de Rome*, site ameliefr.club.fr/Aiglon-Rene-Decq-html.

Delperrié de Bayac, Jacques, *Le Royaume du Maréchal*, Paris, R. Laffont, 1975.

Difrane, Monique, *Du cyprès à l'olivier*, Paris, Gallimard, 1959.

Docteur, Amiral, *La Grande Énigme de la guerre: Darlan amiral de la flotte*, Paris, Éditions de la Couronne, 1949.

Dreyfus, François-Georges, *Histoire de Vichy*, Paris, Éd. De Fallois, 2004.

Drieu La Rochelle, Pierre, *Journal*, 1939–1945, Paris, Hervier Julien, 1992.

Durand, Yves, *Vichy 1940–1944*, Paris, Bordas 1972.

Fabre-Luce, Alfred, *Journal de la France 1939–1944*, Genève, Les Éditions du Cheval ailé, 1946.

Ferro, Marc, *Pétain*, Paris, Hachette, 1987.

Gounelle, Claude, *De Vichy à Montoire*, Paris, Presses de la Cité, 1966.

Griffiths, Richard, *Pétain: a biography of Marshal Philippe Pétain of Vichy*, New York, Garden City, 1972.

Heller, Gerhard, *Un Allemand à Paris*, Paris, Éditions du Seuil, 1981.

Institut Hoover, *La Vie de la France sous l'Occupation*, 2t., Paris, Plon, 1958.

——, *Les Invalides, trois siècles d'Histoire*, Paris, Musée de l'Armée, 1974

Jäckel, E., *La France dans l'Europe d'Hitler*, Paris, 1968.

Jackson, Julian, *La France sous l'Occupation*, Paris, Flammarion, 2004.

Jeantet, Gabriel, *Pétain contre Hitler*, Paris, la Table ronde, 1966.

Joseph, Gilbert, *Fernand de Brinon, l'aristocrate de la Collaboration*, Paris, Albin Michel, 2002.

Kupferman, Fred, *Pierre Laval*, Paris, Masson, 1976 *Laval 1883–1945*, Paris, Balland, 1987

Lambauer, B, *Otto Abetz et les Français: ou l'envers de la Collaboration*, Paris, Fayard, 2001.

Laure, Général, *Pétain*, Paris, Berger-Levrault, 1941.

Lépagnot, Christian, *Histoire de Vichy*, 3 Vols., Genève, Vernoy, 1979.

Lottman, Herbert, *Pétain*, Paris, Éditions du Seuil, 1984

Macé, Jacques. *L'Honneur retrouvé du général de Montholon*, Paris, 2000.

Mallet, Alfred, *Pierre Laval*, 2 vols., Paris, Amiot-Dumont, 1954.

Martin du Gard, Maurice, *La Chronique de Vichy*, Paris, Flammarion, 1948.

Maury, René, *Albine, le dernier amour de Napoléon*, Paris, 1998.

Melton, George E, *Darlan*, Paris, Pygmalion, 2002.

Michel, Henri, *Vichy année quarante*, Paris, R. Laffont, 1966.

Pétain, Laval, Darlan, trois politiques?...., Paris, Flammarion, 1972.

Mordal, Jacques, *Le retour des cendres de l'Aiglon*, Miroir de l'Histoire, décembre 1955.

Moulin de la Barthète, Henri du, *Le Temps des illusions*, Genève, Les Éditions du Cheval ailé, 1946.

Muratori-Philip, Anne, *Histoire des Invalides*, Paris, 2001.

Paxton, R. O., *La France de Vichy: 1940–1944*, Paris, Éditions du Seuil, nouv. ed., 1997.

Peyrouton, Bernard Marcel, *Du service public à la prison commune*, Paris, Plon, 1950.

Plumyène, Jean, *Pétain*, Paris, Éditions du Seuil, 1965.

Poisson, Georges, *L'Aventure du Retour des cendres*, Paris, Tallandier, 2004.

——, *Le retour des cendres de l'Aiglon*, dans *l'Illustration*, 21 décembre 1940.

Stehlin, Paul, *Témoignage pour l'Histoire*, Paris, R. Laffont, 1964.

Stucki, Walter, *Von Pétain zur vierten Republik*, Berne, H. Lang, 1947.

Tournoux, Jean-Raymond, *Pétain et la France*, Paris, Plon, 1980.

Le Royaume d'Otto, Paris, Flammarion, 1982.

Tulard, Jean, *Napoléon II*, Paris, Fayard, 1992.

Ullmann, Bernard, *Lisette de Brinon, ma mère*, Bruxelles, Éd. Complexe, 2004.

Vergez-Chaignon (Bénédicte), *Le Docteur Ménétrel*, Paris, Perrin, 2001.

Vinde, Victor, *La Fin d'une grande puissance?* Lausanne, J. Marguerat, 1942.

OTHER BOOKS BY THE AUTHOR

Fontaines de Paris, Paris, Le Centurion, 1958.

Évocation du Grand Paris, 3 t., Paris, Éditions de Minuit, 1956–1961.

Île-de-France, pays du Dimanche, Paris, Arts et métiers graphiques, 1964.

Châteaux d'Île-de-France, Paris, Balland, 1968.

Le Val-de-Marne, Paris, Éditions de Minuit, 1968. Couronné par l'Académie française.

Album Saint-Simon, Paris, Bibliothèque de la Pléiade, 1969.

Inventaire des églises des Hauts-de-Seine, Paris, Fédération des sociétés historiques, 1973–1975.

Les Musées de France, Paris, coll. Que sais-je?, 3e éd., 1976.

Histoire des Grands boulevards, Paris, Le Cadratin, 1980. Couronné par l'Académie française.

Histoire et histoires de Sceaux, préface de Georges Duhamel, Sceaux, Les Amis du Musée de l'Île de France, 3e éd. 1981.

Dix siècles à Montfort-l'Amaury (avec M. H. Hadrot), préface de Jacques de Lacretelle, Montfort-l'Amaury: s. ed. 1983. Couronné par l'Académie française.

Saint-Simon et le Perche, Mortagne, 1986.

Monte-Cristo, un château de roman, préface d'Alain Decaux, Marly-le-Roi, Champflour, 1987.

Guide des statues de Paris, Paris, Hazan, 1990.

De Maisons sur Seine à Maisons-Laffitte, préface de J. B. Duroselle, Maisons-Laffitte, Association de sauve-garde et de mise en valeur du parc de Maisons-Laffitte, 3e éd. 1993

Les Hauts-de-Seine autrefois, Lyon, Horvath, 3e éd. 1994.

Participation au *Dictionnaire du Second Empire* de Jean Tulard, Paris, Fayard, 1995.

Le Sort des statues de bronze parisiennes sous l'occupation allemande, Paris, Fédération des sociétés historiques, 1996.

Les Maisons d'écrivains, Paris, coll. Que sais-je?, 1997.

Histoire de l'architecture à Paris, Paris, Nouvelle Histoire de Paris, 1997.

La Curieuse Histoire du Vésinet, préface d'Alain Decaux, 3e éd., 1998.

Les Orléans, une famille en quête d'un trône, Paris, Perrin, 3e éd. 1999

La Duchesse de Chevreuse, Paris, Perrin, 1999.

Histoire de l'Élysée, Paris, Perrin. Couronné par l'Académie française. 5e édition sous presse.

Participation au *Dictionnaire Napoléon* de Jean Tulard, Paris, Fayard, 2e éd., 1999.

Monsieur de Saint-Simon, Paris, Flammarion, 5e édition en préparation.

Dictionnaire des monuments d'Île-de-France (dir.) Paris, Hervas, 2e éd. 2004. Couronné par l'association Vieilles maisons françaises.

Maintenon (Avec Françoise Chandernagor), Paris, Norma, 2001.

Les Grands Travaux des présidents de la Ve République, Paris, Parigramme, 2002.

Napoléon et Paris, Tallandier, 2e éd. 2002.

Guide des maisons d'hommes et femmes célèbres, Paris, Pierre Horay, 7e éd. 2003.

Les Gabriel (with Y. Bottineau et M. Gallet), Paris, Picard, 2e éd. 2004.

L'Aventure du Retour des cendres, preface by Jean Tulard, Paris, Tallandier, 2004.

Choderlos de Laclos ou l'obstination, Paris, Grasset, 3e éd. 2005, Bourse Goncourt de la Biographie, 1985.

Index